D0383129

JUICES & SMOOTHIES

Good Housekeeping

JUICES & SMOOTHIES

SENSATIONAL RECIPES TO MAKE IN YOUR BLENDER

★ GOOD FOOD GUARANTEED ★

HEARST BOOKS
New York

HEARST BOOKS
New York

An Imprint of Sterling Publishing
387 Park Avenue South
New York, NY 10016

ISBN 978-1-61837-153-9

Cover Design: Chris Thompson and Yeon Kim
Interior Design: Yeon Kim
Project Editor: Andrea Lynn

The Good Housekeeping Cookbook Seal guarantees that the recipes in this cookbook meet the strict standards of the Good Housekeeping Research Institute. The Institute has been a source of reliable information and a consumer advocate since 1900, and established its seal of approval in 1909. Every recipe has been triple-tested for ease, reliability, and great taste.

For information about custom editions, special sales, and premium and corporate purchases, please contact Sterling Special Sales at 800-805-5489 or specialsales@sterlingpublishing.com.

Distributed in Canada by Sterling Publishing
c/o Canadian Manda Group, 664 Annette Street
Toronto, Ontario, Canada M6S 2C8
Distributed in Australia by Capricorn Link (Australia) Pty. Ltd.
P.O. Box 704, Windsor, NSW 2756, Australia

Printed in Canada

2 4 6 8 10 9 7 5 3

www.sterlingpublishing.com

CONTENTS

Blueberry-Orange Jumpstart Smoothie *(page 30)*

Foreword

The test kitchen was literally buzzing as we created the recipes for *Good Housekeeping Juices & Smoothies*. We had a lot of fun plotting, blending and tasting. And why not? The blender makes it easy to cook just about anything—simply press the button and buzz. There's little cleanup and most of the recipes are so simple, even kids can help by throwing ingredients into the blender. Better yet, almost every recipe in this book is a treat by anyone's definition—luscious smoothies, blender juices, soda fountain creations, creamy soups, and some very delicious frozen cocktails.

Juices & Smoothies also addresses our time-crunched schedules. Like many of us you may be short on time but still wants to make delicious, nutritious food for your family. If you want to get the kids off to school in minutes, give them one of our creamy smoothies made with yogurt, milk, or soy milk. They are protein-packed and flavorful. Imagine starting the day with a Powered-Up Purple Smoothie, Breakfast Jumpstart, or Sunrise Smoothie! Enhance a smoothie with flaxseeds, oats, or wheat germ for extra on-the-go oomph.

Looking for a special treat to share? Indulge the after-school crowd with a Double-Chocolate Malted Milkshake, Classic Vanilla Milkshake, or Root Beer Float. For an afternoon pick-me-up, try our Frosty Cappuccino and Mocha Frappa Cinno—we think they're just as good as their coffee bar rivals.

Want to make colorful cocktails just like the ones at your favorite watering hole? Frozen Cocktails and Slushes is where you'll discover how easy (and delicious), it is to prepare daiquiris, margaritas, and piña coladas, plus sensational nonalcoholic beverages such as our Frozen Virgin Mary and Frozen Iced Tea.

Your blender will make quick work of fixing soup, too. You'll find smoothy silky-textured soups, like Cream of Broccoli or Roasted Carrot Soup. You'll also discover how easy it is to make a perfect, foolproof Hollandaise Sauce and to wow guests at the next potluck party with Black Bean Dip.

So get ready to enjoy some of the easiest, most delicious recipes you've ever tasted—with just the push of a button, it's that simple. It's also fun—so why not get started now!

SUSAN WESTMORELAND
Food Director, *Good Housekeeping*

The Buzz on Blenders

Icy cold drinks, velvety soups, creamy soda fountain treats—you can make them all quickly and easily in the blender with just the flick of the wrist. However, to ensure perfect results every time, and for safety's sake, it helps to know a little bit about how your blender works and to follow a few simple food-preparation guidelines.

SPEEDING PERMITTED

All blenders feature a control panel offering several speed options. Some models have four or five speeds, others just high and low; still other manufacturers list methods rather than speed, such as whip, puree, liquefy, chop. But rest assured—you can make any recipe in this book in any standard blender using the high button, which blends foods quickly and smoothly. If your blender has a puree button, which is more powerful, use it for making thicker mixtures such as soups and dips. You can use the high button for soups and dips, too—it will just take a bit longer.

SAFETY DOES IT

- Always keep your hand on top of the blender while it is in use as a precaution against the top coming off unexpectedly. This can happen if you've added too many ingredients at one time or when they create more volume than you anticipated.
- Be sure the motor is off before you scrape down the sides of the blender to move the food onto the blades. Use a rubber spatula only—not a metal one or a knife.
- Never put your fingers in the container. The blades are sharp.

BLEND IT BETTER

Whether you're making a silky-smooth soup or a frozen slush, the goal when blending is always the same—consistent texture.

- Add the food in small batches. This will ensure that your ingredients get uniformly pureed and keep the blender from overflowing.
- Chill the ingredients before making blender drinks. This will keep your drinks cold longer.
- Cut pieces of fruit and vegetables into small uniform sizes. This gives better consistency and puts less strain on the blender motor.
- Place equal parts liquid and solid foods in the blender when pureeing soups. This will keep the texture consistent from one batch to the next.
- For best texture, let hot liquids cool slightly before adding them to the blender.
- Always crush ice or break it into small cubes before adding it to the container, particularly if your blender has a less powerful motor.
- If you are blending ice with other ingredients, add ice to the blender last.

BUYING A NEW BLENDER

Once you discover the wonderful variety of luscious smoothies, frozen drinks, soups, and dips that can be made in the blender, you may want to buy a newer, bigger, and more powerful model. If so, check the options out carefully before you make your purchase.

- Look for a blender that has a sturdy base to keep it stable. This will prevent it from jumping around on the counter while in use.
- Check the capacity of the glass or plastic container. A smaller (32-ounce) container is fine if you will be making just one smoothie or drink at a time. However, opt for a 40-ounce container if you plan to whip up two drinks at a time or blend soups.
- Consider paying extra for a more powerful motor, particularly if you will be making slushes and frozen cocktails. Many of the newer blenders have up to 1000-watt motors that make crushing ice a snap.

Roasted Carrot Soup (page 102)

Banana, Berry, and Pineapple Smoothie *(page 14)*

1 Fruit Smoothies & Blender Breakfasts

Turn to the blender for easy and healthy breakfast needs, our favorite no-fuss approach to the morning meal. Make sure to stock your freezer with fruit (buy it frozen, or shop fresh and freeze), keep fresh produce on hand, and stock fruit juices in the fridge. Then the sky is the limit in terms of smoothie selections in the morning.

Breakfast Jumpstart whirls together strawberries, banana, soy milk, and wheat germ, while kale bulks up the antioxidant-fueled Powered-Up Purple Smoothie. Carrot juice is the healthy sweetening secret in Pineapple-Citrus Smoothie and oats bring nutritional heft to Berry-Banana Smoothie. Don't forget that these frosty fruit drinks also make the perfect afternoon pick-me-up—try the grape-packed Green Thumb Smoothie or the tropical Papaya Punch.

Apricot-Raspberry REFRESHER

A delicious ruby-red razzle dazzler. Top it with some fresh berries.

ACTIVE TIME: 5 MINUTES **TOTAL TIME:** 5 MINUTES **MAKES:** 1 SERVING OR 1¾ CUPS

- 1 can (5.5 ounces) apricot nectar, chilled (⅔ cup)
- ½ can (15 ounces) apricot halves in light syrup, drained (7 to 8 halves)
- 3 ice cubes
- 1 tablespoon honey
- ⅔ cup frozen raspberries

In blender, combine apricot nectar, apricot halves, ice, and honey and blend until mixture is smooth. Add raspberries and blend until broken up but not completely blended in. Pour into 1 tall glass.

EACH SERVING: ABOUT 262 CALORIES, 2G PROTEIN, 68G CARBOHYDRATE, 0G TOTAL FAT (0G SATURATED), 0MG CHOLESTEROL, 12MG SODIUM.

Tropical Mango SMOOTHIE

Paradise in a glass. Make it with a firm ripe banana for the best flavor.

ACTIVE TIME: 10 MINUTES **TOTAL TIME:** 10 MINUTES **MAKES:** 1 SERVING OR 2 CUPS

- ½ cup pineapple juice, chilled
- 1 cup diced mango
- 1 banana, sliced
- 2 teaspoons fresh lime juice
- ½ teaspoon grated, peeled fresh ginger (see tip, page 45)
- 3 ice cubes

In blender, combine pineapple juice, mango, banana, lime juice, ginger, and ice and blend until mixture is smooth. Pour into 1 tall glass.

EACH SERVING: ABOUT 289 CALORIES, 3G PROTEIN, 74G CARBOHYDRATE, 1G TOTAL FAT (0G SATURATED), 0MG CHOLESTEROL, 6MG SODIUM.

Apricot-Raspberry Refresher

Banana, Berry, and Pineapple SMOOTHIE

Ginger gives a spicy boost to this fruit smoothie. Photo on page 10.

ACTIVE TIME: 10 MINUTES **TOTAL TIME:** 10 MINUTES **MAKES:** 2 SERVINGS OR 3¼ CUPS

- 1 small banana
- ¾ cup pineapple juice
- ½ cup ice cubes
- 1 cup blueberries
- 1 cup raspberries or blackberries
- 2 teaspoons honey
- 1 teaspoon grated, peeled fresh ginger (see tip, page 45)

In blender, puree banana, pineapple juice, ice, blueberries, raspberries or blackberries, honey, and ginger until smooth.

EACH SERVING: ABOUT 190 CALORIES, 2G PROTEIN, 47G CARBOHYDRATE, 1G TOTAL FAT (0G SATURATED), 0MG CHOLESTEROL, 30MG SODIUM.

Breakfast JUMPSTART

As healthy a morning lift off as you could find! This luscious blend of soy milk, fruits, and a sprinkling of wheat germ is loaded with vitamins and minerals to get you going. Low-fat milk or almond milk can be subbed for the soy milk.

ACTIVE TIME: 5 MINUTES **TOTAL TIME:** 5 MINUTES **MAKES:** 1 SERVING OR 2 CUPS

1 cup soy milk
1 frozen banana, sliced
1 cup strawberries, hulled
2 tablespoons wheat germ
1 tablespoon honey

In blender, combine soy milk, banana, strawberries, wheat germ, and honey. Blend until mixture is smooth and frothy. Pour into 1 tall glass.

EACH SERVING: ABOUT 342 CALORIES, 13G PROTEIN, 66G CARBOHYDRATE, 7G TOTAL FAT (0G SATURATED), 0MG CHOLESTEROL, 33MG SODIUM.

Sunrise SMOOTHIE

Start your day with this tropical blend of pineapple, banana, and orange juice.

ACTIVE TIME: 10 MINUTES **TOTAL TIME:** 10 MINUTES **MAKES:** 4 SERVINGS

1 banana
2 cups ice cubes
2 cups frozen pineapple chunks
1 cup orange juice
½ cup vanilla yogurt

In blender, puree banana, ice, pineapple, orange juice, and yogurt. Blend until mixture is smooth and frothy. Pour into 4 glasses.

EACH SERVING: ABOUT 121 CALORIES, 3G PROTEIN, 28G CARBOHYDRATE, 1G TOTAL FAT (0G SATURATED), 1MG CHOLESTEROL, 22MG SODIUM.

Cantaloupe-Lime Smoothie

Cantaloupe-Lime SMOOTHIE

Double your pleasure and make two. Garnish with a fresh slice of lime.

ACTIVE TIME: 10 MINUTES **TOTAL TIME:** 10 MINUTES **MAKES:** 1 SERVING OR 2 CUPS

- 1 lime
- 2 cups diced cantaloupe
- ⅓ cup diced peach
- 1 tablespoon honey
- 3 ice cubes

1 From lime, grate ½ teaspoon peel and squeeze 2 tablespoons juice.

2 In blender, combine grated lime peel, lime juice, cantaloupe, peach, honey, and ice; blend until mixture is smooth and frothy. Pour into 1 tall glass.

EACH SERVING: ABOUT 233 CALORIES, 4G PROTEIN, 60G CARBOHYDRATE, 1G TOTAL FAT (0G SATURATED), 0MG CHOLESTEROL, 30MG SODIUM.

Green Thumb SMOOTHIE

An icy sparkler that tastes like it came straight from the garden.

ACTIVE TIME: 10 MINUTES PLUS FREEZING **TOTAL TIME:** 10 MINUTES **MAKES:** 1 SERVING OR 1¾ CUPS

- ½ cup white grape juice, chilled
- 1 cup frozen seedless green grapes
- 1 cup seeded, diced cucumber

In blender, combine grape juice, grapes, and cucumber and blend until mixture is smooth. Pour into 1 tall glass.

EACH SERVING: ABOUT 205 CALORIES, 2G PROTEIN, 50G CARBOHYDRATE, 1G TOTAL FAT (0G SATURATED), 0MG CHOLESTEROL, 9MG SODIUM.

Honeydew-Kiwi COOLER

A refreshing mix of melon and kiwi that's also good for you. Kiwis have even more vitamin C than oranges.

ACTIVE TIME: 10 MINUTES **TOTAL TIME:** 10 MINUTES **MAKES:** 1 SERVING OR 2 CUPS

- 2 cups diced honeydew melon
- 1 tablespoon fresh lemon juice
- 1 tablespoon honey
- 3 ice cubes
- ½ cup frozen diced kiwi (see tip)

In blender, combine honeydew, lemon juice, honey, and ice and blend until smooth. Add kiwi and blend until kiwi is broken up, but the seeds are not ground. Pour into 1 tall glass.

EACH SERVING: ABOUT 246 CALORIES, 3G PROTEIN, 64G CARBOHYDRATE, 1G TOTAL FAT (0G SATURATED), 0MG CHOLESTEROL, 41MG SODIUM.

With a sharp knife or a swivel vegetable peeler, peel off kiwi skin. Or, cut unpeeled kiwi in half crosswise and use a spoon to remove the fruit's flesh from its peel.

Powered-Up Purple SMOOTHIE

Boost your morning routine with this antioxidant-rich smoothie. Berries, kale, and flax amp the iron, calcium, vitamin A, and vitamin C.

ACTIVE TIME: 10 MINUTES **TOTAL TIME:** 10 MINUTES **MAKES:** 1 SERVING

½ cup fat-free milk
½ cup nonfat Greek yogurt
⅔ cup kale
1 cup blueberries
1 teaspoon ground flaxseed (see tip, opposite)
1 teaspoon honey

In blender, combine milk, yogurt, kale, blueberries, ground flaxseed, and honey. Blend until mixture is smooth. Pour into 1 tall glass.

EACH SERVING: ABOUT 242 CALORIES, 18G PROTEIN, 42G CARBOHYDRATE, 1G TOTAL FAT (0G SATURATED), 2MG CHOLESTEROL, 113MG SODIUM.

Papaya PUNCH

This papaya-packed punch is rich in beta-carotene.

ACTIVE TIME: 10 MINUTES **TOTAL TIME:** 10 MINUTES **MAKES:** 1 SERVING OR 1½ CUPS

1 cup papaya nectar or orange juice, chilled
1 cup diced papaya
1 tablespoon fresh lime juice
1 to 2 teaspoons sugar
1 drop coconut extract
3 ice cubes

In blender, combine papaya nectar, papaya, lime juice, sugar, coconut extract, and ice and blend until mixture is smooth. Pour into 1 tall glass.

EACH SERVING: ABOUT 232 CALORIES, 1G PROTEIN, 59G CARBOHYDRATE, 1G TOTAL FAT (0G SATURATED), 0MG CHOLESTEROL, 17MG SODIUM.

Health-Nut SMOOTHIE

So good-tasting and so good for you. In addition to vitamin-rich blueberries and apples, this elixir contains flaxseed, a rich source of omega-3 fatty acids, fiber, minerals, and amino acids.

ACTIVE TIME: 10 MINUTES **TOTAL TIME:** 10 MINUTES **MAKES:** 1 SERVING OR 1¾ CUPS

1 navel orange
½ cup plain low-fat yogurt
⅔ cup frozen blueberries
½ cup chopped apple
3 ice cubes
1 to 2 tablespoons honey
1 to 2 tablespoons ground flaxseed (see tip)
granola for garnish

1 From orange, grate ½ teaspoon peel. Remove remaining peel and white pith from orange and discard. Section orange.

2 In blender, combine orange peel, orange sections, yogurt, blueberries, apple, ice, honey, and flaxseed and blend until mixture is smooth. Pour into 1 tall glass. Garnish with granola.

EACH SERVING: ABOUT 424 CALORIES, 11G PROTEIN, 84G CARBOHYDRATE, 7G TOTAL FAT (2G SATURATED), 7MG CHOLESTEROL, 106MG SODIUM.

Although you can buy ground flaxseed, the advantage to buying it whole is that it will stay at its optimum freshness. To release the heart-healthy nutrients from its hard shell, it must be ground in a blender or in a nut or coffee grinder before it is added to the smoothie.

Apple-Banana SMOOTHIE

Here's an easy and delicious way to get your apple a day. We used a Granny Smith, but you could substitute a Golden Delicious or Gala, if you prefer.

ACTIVE TIME: 10 MINUTES **TOTAL TIME:** 10 MINUTES **MAKES:** 1 SERVING OR 2 CUPS

¾ cup apple juice, chilled
¼ cup frozen apple juice concentrate
⅓ cup applesauce
1 cup frozen diced Granny Smith apple
½ frozen banana, sliced
pinch ground cardamom

In a blender, combine apple juice, apple juice concentrate, applesauce, diced apple, banana, and cardamom and blend until mixture is smooth. Pour into 1 tall glass.

EACH SERVING: ABOUT 387 CALORIES, 1G PROTEIN, 98G CARBOHYDRATE, 1G TOTAL FAT (0G SATURATED), 0MG CHOLESTEROL, 26MG SODIUM.

Ginger-Peach BLUSH

This sensational smoothie gets its gorgeous color from raspberries and its zip from candied ginger.

ACTIVE TIME: 5 MINUTES **TOTAL TIME:** 5 MINUTES **MAKES:** 1 SERVING OR 1¾ CUPS

1 cup peach nectar, chilled
1 cup frozen sliced peaches
¼ cup frozen raspberries
2 teaspoons minced crystallized ginger

In blender, combine peach nectar, peaches, raspberries, and ginger and blend until mixture is smooth. Pour into 1 tall glass.

EACH SERVING: ABOUT 244 CALORIES, 2G PROTEIN, 63G CARBOHYDRATE, 0G TOTAL FAT (0G SATURATED), 0MG CHOLESTEROL, 19MG SODIUM.

Wake-Up Orange SMOOTHIE

What a way to start the day! If you don't have soy milk, you can substitute low-fat milk or buttermilk.

ACTIVE TIME: 5 MINUTES **TOTAL TIME:** 5 MINUTES **MAKES:** 1 SERVING OR 1¾ CUPS

- 1 cup vanilla soy milk
- ¼ cup frozen orange juice concentrate
- 2 tablespoons orange marmalade
- 2 ice cubes

In blender, combine soy milk, orange juice concentrate, marmalade, and ice cubes. Blend until mixture is smooth and frothy. Pour into 1 tall glass.

EACH SERVING: ABOUT 360 CALORIES, 8G PROTEIN, 73G CARBOHYDRATE, 5G TOTAL FAT (0G SATURATED), 0MG CHOLESTEROL, 144MG SODIUM.

Pineapple-Citrus SMOOTHIE

Sunshine in a glass! And it's a nutritional knockout to boot. The orange juice and pineapple are high in Vitamin C and the banana is a good source of potassium.

ACTIVE TIME: 5 MINUTES **TOTAL TIME:** 5 MINUTES **MAKES:** 1 SERVING OR 1¾ CUPS

- ¾ cup orange-tangerine juice blend, chilled
- ¼ cup carrot juice, chilled
- 1 cup frozen canned pineapple chunks
- ½ frozen banana, sliced

In blender, combine orange-tangerine juice, carrot juice, pineapple, and banana and blend until mixture is smooth and frothy. Pour into 1 tall glass.

EACH SERVING: ABOUT 285 CALORIES, 1G PROTEIN, 72G CARBOHYDRATE, 0G TOTAL FAT (0G SATURATED), 0MG CHOLESTEROL, 40MG SODIUM.

Berry-Banana SMOOTHIE

Oats aren't just for oatmeal-making anymore. They add body and fiber to help keep hunger away.

ACTIVE TIME: 10 MINUTES **TOTAL TIME:** 10 MINUTES **MAKES:** 4 SERVINGS

- 2 cups frozen strawberries
- 1 cup low-fat vanilla yogurt
- 1 banana, sliced
- ½ cup oats
- ½ cup orange juice
- 2 tablespoons honey

In blender, combine strawberries, yogurt, banana, oats, orange juice, and honey. Blend until mixture is smooth. Pour into 4 glasses.

EACH SERVING: ABOUT 190 CALORIES, 6G PROTEIN, 41G CARBOHYDRATE, 2G TOTAL FAT (0G SATURATED), 3MG CHOLESTEROL, 43MG SODIUM.

Blueberry Blast
(page 39)

2 Yogurt & Dairy-Based Smoothies

Yogurt adds a divine creaminess to this chapter's smoothie selections, whether it's for the berry-peach combo of Strawberries and Cream or the goodness of the Great Grape Smoothie. The lactose intolerant need not skip these creations. Just make purchase lactose-free yogurt instead. Soy milk, almond milk, or even lactose-free milk can be swapped out where milk is used.

Banana Bayou Smoothie plus Black and Blueberry Blizzard get a tart, vitamin-heavy lift from buttermilk. Flavored yogurt offers an extra oomph of flavor, like blueberry yogurt in Blueberry Blast, strawberry yogurt in Strawberry Mania, and lemon yogurt in Lemon-Cranberry Smoothie.

Also consider smoothies for an end-of-the-evening dessert treat. Who wouldn't be thrilled with the sweetness of the Chocolate-Banana Smoothie or the tropical beach quality of a Piña Colada Smoothie?

Strawberries AND CREAM

Peaches meld with vanilla frozen yogurt and berries for a delicious frothy experience.

ACTIVE TIME: 10 MINUTES **TOTAL TIME:** 10 MINUTES **MAKES:** 2 SERVINGS

- 1 pound strawberries, hulled
- 1 cup frozen peach slices
- ¼ cup low-fat vanilla frozen yogurt
- ¼ cup skim milk
- 2 tablespoons honey

In blender, puree strawberries, peach slices, frozen yogurt, milk, and honey until smooth. Pour into 2 glasses.

EACH SERVING: ABOUT 217 CALORIES, 5G PROTEIN, 50G CARBOHYDRATE, 2G TOTAL FAT (1G SATURATED), 17MG CHOLESTEROL, 30MG SODIUM.

Banana Bayou SMOOTHIE

As rich and delicious as that other Big Easy favorite—Bananas Foster.

ACTIVE TIME: 5 MINUTES **TOTAL TIME:** 5 MINUTES **MAKES:** 1 SERVING OR 1½ CUPS

- 1 cup buttermilk
- 1 frozen banana, sliced
- 2 tablespoons prepared caramel sauce
- 1 tablespoon chopped pecans for garnish

In blender, combine buttermilk, banana, and caramel sauce and blend until mixture is smooth and frothy. Pour into 1 tall glass and garnish with pecans.

EACH SERVING: ABOUT 384 CALORIES, 10G PROTEIN, 71G CARBOHYDRATE, 8G TOTAL FAT (2G SATURATED), 9MG CHOLESTEROL, 368MG SODIUM.

Lemon-Cranberry SMOOTHIE

This classy, cool combo is perfect for a hot summer day.

ACTIVE TIME: 10 MINUTES **TOTAL TIME:** 10 MINUTES **MAKES:** 1 SERVING OR 2 CUPS

- 1 to 2 lemons
- 1 container (8 ounces) low-fat lemon yogurt
- ½ cup whole-berry cranberry sauce, chilled
- 4 to 5 ice cubes

1 From lemons, grate 1 teaspoon peel and squeeze 3 tablespoons juice.

2 In blender, combine lemon peel, lemon juice, yogurt, cranberry sauce, and ice and blend until mixture is smooth. Pour into 1 tall glass.

EACH SERVING: ABOUT 442 CALORIES, 10G PROTEIN, 96G CARBOHYDRATE, 3G TOTAL FAT (2G SATURATED), 15MG CHOLESTEROL, 230MG SODIUM.

Blueberry-Orange
JUMPSTART SMOOTHIE

You can substitute the same quantity of fresh or frozen blackberries, raspberries, or even chopped mango in this gingery smoothie.

ACTIVE TIME: 5 MINUTES **TOTAL TIME:** 5 MINUTES **MAKES:** 2 SERVINGS

- 1 cup frozen strawberries
- ½ cup fresh blueberries
- ½ cup fresh orange juice
- 2 teaspoons grated, peeled fresh ginger (see tip, page 45)
- ¼ cup plain low-fat yogurt
- 2 ice cubes

In blender, combine strawberries, blueberries, orange juice, ginger, yogurt, and ice cubes. Blend until smooth, scraping down side of container occasionally. Pour into 2 tall glasses and serve.

EACH SERVING: ABOUT 90 CALORIES, 3G PROTEIN, 21G CARBOHYDRATE, 1G TOTAL FAT (0G SATURATED), 2MG CHOLESTEROL, 25MG SODIUM.

Mango-Strawberry Smoothie

Mango-Strawberry SMOOTHIE

Either way you make it—with mango nectar or with apricot nectar—this is a wonderful combination. If you use frozen berries, skip the ice cubes.

ACTIVE TIME: 5 MINUTES **TOTAL TIME:** 5 MINUTES **MAKES:** 2 SERVINGS OR 2½ CUPS

- 1 cup fresh strawberries or frozen unsweetened strawberries
- 1 cup mango or apricot nectar, chilled
- ½ cup plain or vanilla yogurt
- 4 ice cubes

In blender, combine strawberries, mango nectar, yogurt, and ice and blend until mixture is smooth and frothy. Pour into 2 tall glasses.

EACH SERVING: ABOUT 129 CALORIES, 4G PROTEIN, 27G CARBOHYDRATE, 1G TOTAL FAT (1G SATURATED), 3MG CHOLESTEROL, 44MG SODIUM.

Black and Blueberry BLIZZARD

This spectacular blend is vitamin packed—and low-fat, too.

ACTIVE TIME: 5 MINUTES **TOTAL TIME:** 5 MINUTES **MAKES:** 1 SERVING OR 2 CUPS

- ½ cup buttermilk
- ½ cup orange juice, chilled
- 1 cup frozen blueberries
- ½ cup frozen blackberries
- 1 tablespoon honey

In blender, combine buttermilk, orange juice, blueberries, blackberries, and honey and blend until mixture is smooth and frothy. Pour into 1 tall glass.

EACH SERVING: ABOUT 287 CALORIES, 7G PROTEIN, 64G CARBOHYDRATE, 2G TOTAL FAT (1G SATURATED), 4MG CHOLESTEROL, 141MG SODIUM.

Strawberry MANIA

A hint of cranberry juice makes this pink drink doubly delicious.

ACTIVE TIME: 5 MINUTES **TOTAL TIME:** 5 MINUTES **MAKES:** 1 SERVING OR 1¾ CUPS

- ¼ cup cranberry juice cocktail, chilled
- 1 container (8 ounces) low-fat strawberry yogurt
- 1 cup frozen strawberries

In blender, combine cranberry juice, yogurt, and strawberries and blend until mixture is smooth and frothy. Pour into 1 tall glass.

EACH SERVING: ABOUT 326 CALORIES, 10G PROTEIN, 68G CARBOHYDRATE, 4G TOTAL FAT (2G SATURATED), 15MG CHOLESTEROL, 141MG SODIUM.

Double-Peach SMOOTHIE

Be sure to use juicy, ripe peaches for the best flavor.

ACTIVE TIME: 5 MINUTES **TOTAL TIME:** 5 MINUTES **MAKES:** 2 SERVINGS OR 2¾ CUPS

- 1 cup peeled, sliced peaches (about 2 medium)
- 1 cup peach juice or nectar, chilled
- ½ cup vanilla low-fat yogurt
- 3 ice cubes

In blender, combine peaches, peach juice, yogurt, and ice and blend until mixture is smooth and frothy. Pour into 2 tall glasses.

EACH SERVING: ABOUT 160 CALORIES, 3G PROTEIN, 36G CARBOHYDRATE, 1G TOTAL FAT (1G SATURATED), 3MG CHOLESTEROL, 45MG SODIUM.

Strawberry Mania

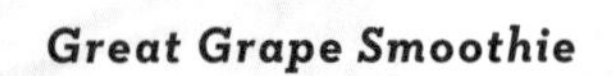

Great Grape Smoothie

Great Grape SMOOTHIE

Here's an especially heart-healthy drink. Not only is it low in fat, but red grapes contain the same phytochemicals found in red wine that protect against heart disease.

ACTIVE TIME: 5 MINUTES **TOTAL TIME:** 5 MINUTES **MAKES:** 1 SERVING OR 1½ CUPS

- ½ cup grape juice, chilled
- ¼ cup plain low-fat yogurt
- 1 cup frozen seedless red grapes

In blender, combine grape juice, yogurt, and grapes and blend until mixture is smooth and frothy. Pour into 1 tall glass.

EACH SERVING: ABOUT 228 CALORIES, 5G PROTEIN, 51G CARBOHYDRATE, 2G TOTAL FAT (1G SATURATED), 4MG CHOLESTEROL, 50MG SODIUM.

Cherry-Berry SMOOTHIE

There are many juice blends available and all would work well in this frosty drink. We used one that is a combination of carrot, apple, cherry, and three berry juices.

ACTIVE TIME: 5 MINUTES **TOTAL TIME:** 5 MINUTES **MAKES:** 1 SERVING OR 2 CUPS

- ½ cup berry juice blend, chilled
- 1 container (8 ounces) low-fat cherry yogurt
- ½ cup frozen pitted sweet cherries
- 2 ice cubes

In a blender, combine juice, yogurt, cherries, and ice and blend until mixture is smooth and frothy. Pour into 1 tall glass.

EACH SERVING: ABOUT 410 CALORIES, 10G PROTEIN, 87G CARBOHYDRATE, 3G TOTAL FAT (2G SATURATED), 15MG CHOLESTEROL, 159MG SODIUM.

Chocolate-Banana SMOOTHIE

Kids love the combo of chocolate and bananas, and it's so easy to make, they can do it themselves.

ACTIVE TIME: 5 MINUTES **TOTAL TIME:** 5 MINUTES **MAKES:** 1 SERVING OR 2 CUPS

1 frozen banana, sliced (see tip)
¾ cup milk
3 to 4 tablespoons chocolate syrup
3 to 4 ice cubes

In blender, combine banana, milk, chocolate syrup, and ice and blend until mixture is smooth and frothy. Pour into 1 tall glass.

EACH SERVING: ABOUT 430 CALORIES, 9G PROTEIN, 85G CARBOHYDRATE, 8G TOTAL FAT (4G SATURATED), 25MG CHOLESTEROL, 145MG SODIUM.

Using frozen bananas yields a thicker, colder smoothie. Cut peeled banana into chunks and freeze up to a week in a self-sealing plastic bag.

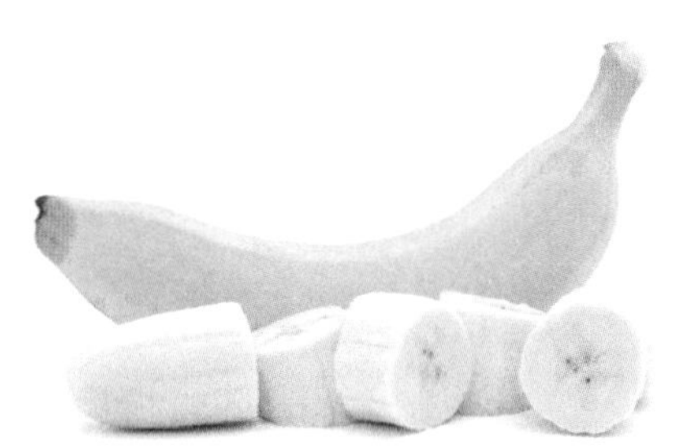

Blueberry BLAST

Garnish with a skewer of fresh blueberries. Photo on page 26.

ACTIVE TIME: 5 MINUTES **TOTAL TIME:** 5 MINUTES **MAKES:** 1 SERVING OR 1⅓ CUPS

- ¼ cup cranberry juice cocktail, chilled
- 1 container (8 ounces) low-fat blueberry yogurt
- ½ cup frozen blueberries

In blender, combine cranberry juice, yogurt, and blueberries and blend until mixture is smooth and frothy. Pour into 1 tall glass.

EACH SERVING: ABOUT 311 CALORIES, 10G PROTEIN, 63G CARBOHYDRATE, 3G TOTAL FAT (2G SATURATED), 15MG CHOLESTEROL, 146MG SODIUM.

Piña Colada SMOOTHIE

Transport yourself beachside with this pineapple and coconut milk smoothie.

ACTIVE TIME: 10 MINUTES **TOTAL TIME:** 10 MINUTES **MAKES:** 4 SERVINGS

- 1 can (20 ounces) pineapple
- 1 banana, ripe
- 1 can (14 ounces) light coconut milk
- 1 container (6 ounces) fat-free vanilla yogurt
- 1 cup ice cubes

In blender, combine pineapple, banana, coconut milk, yogurt, and ice cubes. Blend until mixture is smooth and frothy. Pour into 4 glasses.

EACH SERVING: ABOUT 327 CALORIES, 5G PROTEIN, 38G CARBOHYDRATE, 6G TOTAL FAT (6G SATURATED), 1MG CHOLESTEROL, 44MG SODIUM.

Three-Berry SMOOTHIE

Enjoy the taste of summer year-round with this frosted fruity drink.

ACTIVE TIME: 5 MINUTES **TOTAL TIME:** 5 MINUTES **MAKES:** 1 SERVING OR 1¼ CUPS

- ½ cup cranberry-raspberry juice, chilled
- ½ cup low-fat vanilla yogurt
- 1 cup frozen berry medley (strawberries, raspberries, blackberries, and blueberries)
- 2 teaspoons honey

In blender, combine cranberry-raspberry juice, yogurt, berries, and honey and blend until mixture is smooth. Pour into 1 tall glass.

EACH SERVING: ABOUT 293 CALORIES, 7G PROTEIN, 65G CARBOHYDRATE, 2G TOTAL FAT (1G SATURATED), 8MG CHOLESTEROL, 108MG SODIUM.

Creamy Strawberry-Orange SMOOTHIE

This quick fix is a great way to get the kids off to school in the morning.

ACTIVE TIME: 5 MINUTES **TOTAL TIME:** 5 MINUTES **MAKES:** 1 SERVING OR 1¾ CUPS

- ¾ cup orange juice, chilled
- ¼ cup nonfat dry milk
- 1¼ cups frozen strawberries
- 2 tablespoons honey
- 2 ice cubes

In blender, combine orange juice, dry milk, strawberries, honey, and ice and blend until mixture is smooth. Pour into 1 tall glass.

EACH SERVING: ABOUT 338 CALORIES, 8G PROTEIN, 80G CARBOHYDRATE, 1G TOTAL FAT (0G SATURATED), 3MG CHOLESTEROL, 102MG SODIUM.

Green Light (page 45)

3 Blender Juices

Here's a good news flash for homemade juice fans—a juicer isn't always required. All the recipes in this chapter use the mighty blender to create healthy, silky-smooth fruit- and vegetable-based juices. Recipes like the Green Light with kale and Lean, Mean, and Green with spinach add a step of straining the juice at the end to remove pulp while others are ready straight from the blender.

In our sampler of juices, a chunk of fresh ginger invigorates Green Light, coconut milk gives body to Tropical Carrot Tango, and tomatoes meld with fruits in Iced Tomato-Mango Juice and Citrusy Gazpacho Sipper. Other combinations include tart rhubarb and sweet raspberries in Spring in a Glass or herbs and watermelon in Pink Basil Blend. Whether adding one of these juices to your morning breakfast or as an afternoon snack, the juice offerings in this chapter bring creative and nutritious options to the table.

Peachy-Cantaloupe JUICE

Be sure to use the ripest, most fragrant melon you can find.

ACTIVE TIME: 15 MINUTES **TOTAL TIME:** 15 MINUTES **MAKES:** 5 SERVINGS OR 4 CUPS

1 large cantaloupe (2½ pounds), chilled
1 cup peach nectar or apricot nectar, chilled
1 tablespoon fresh lime juice
Lime slices for garnish (optional)

1 Cut cantaloupe in half. Scoop out and discard seeds. Cut away rind, then cut cantaloupe into bite-size pieces.

2 In blender, puree cantaloupe, peach nectar, and lime juice until smooth. Increase speed to high; blend 1 minute. Garnish with lime slices, if desired.

EACH SERVING: ABOUT 67 CALORIES, 1G PROTEIN, 17G CARBOHYDRATE, 0G TOTAL FAT (0G SATURATED), 0MG CHOLESTEROL, 14MG SODIUM.

Iced Tomato-Mango JUICE

Strawberries and carrots add sweetness and nutritional bulk to this blend. For the best flavor use a juicy vine-ripened tomato.

ACTIVE TIME: 10 MINUTES **TOTAL TIME:** 10 MINUTES PLUS FREEZING **MAKES:** 1 SERVING OR 1¾ CUPS

¾ cup carrot juice, chilled
¾ cup diced frozen tomato
¾ cup frozen strawberries
½ cup diced mango

In blender, combine carrot juice, tomato, strawberries, and mango. Blend until mixture is smooth. Pour into 1 tall glass.

EACH SERVING: ABOUT 193 CALORIES, 4G PROTEIN, 47G CARBOHYDRATE, 2G TOTAL FAT (0G SATURATED), 0MG CHOLESTEROL, 71MG SODIUM.

Green Light

Kale is a powerhouse of vitamins and nutrients like vitamin A, vitamin C, and calcium. The bite of these greens is combined with refreshing coconut water and grapes for a blender juice just asking to start any morning routine. Photo on page 42.

ACTIVE TIME: 5 MINUTES **TOTAL TIME:** 5 MINUTES **MAKES:** 1 SERVING OR 1¼ CUPS

- 4 leaves kale, stems and tough ribs removed and discarded
- 1 cup coconut water
- 1 cup seedless green grapes
- 1 small (½-inch) piece fresh peeled ginger (see tip), sliced

1 In blender, combine kale, coconut water, grapes, and ginger until mixture is smooth.

2 Strain through a fine sieve into a large measuring cup; discard pulp. Pour into 1 tall glass.

EACH SERVING: ABOUT 180 CALORIES, 4G PROTEIN, 41G CARBOHYDRATES, 1G TOTAL FAT (0G SATURATED), 0MG CHOLESTEROL, 45MG SODIUM.

To peel ginger, use a vegetable peeler or the edge of a teaspoon to scrape away the thin skin. Be careful to only remove the very top layer of skin because the flesh directly beneath is the youngest and most delicate.

Tropical Carrot TANGO

This much-loved veggie gets a vibrant, tropical makeover with the addition of coconut milk, ginger, and pineapple in this zesty drink.

ACTIVE TIME: 10 MINUTES **TOTAL TIME:** 10 MINUTES **MAKES:** 2 SERVINGS OR 2¼ CUPS

- 1 cup unsweetened light coconut milk
- 1 cup frozen pineapple chunks
- ¾ cup freshly grated peeled carrot
- ¼ cup cold water
- 1 (½-inch) piece fresh peeled ginger (see tip, page 45), sliced
- 1 teaspoon agave nectar (see tip)

In blender, combine coconut milk, pineapple, carrot, water, ginger, and agave until smooth. Pour into 2 tall glasses.

EACH SERVING: EACH SERVING: ABOUT 150 CALORIES, 3G PROTEIN, 20G CARBOHYDRATES, 7G TOTAL FAT (7G SATURATED), 0MG CHOLESTEROL, 40MG SODIUM.

TIP

Don't have any nectar? Don't worry. Honey or even maple syrup can be used as an agave nectar substitute.

Citrusy Gazpacho SIPPER

The tomato-based soup is the inspiration for this blender juice which adds in the sweetness of freshly-squeezed orange juice.

ACTIVE TIME: 5 MINUTES **TOTAL TIME:** 5 MINUTES PLUS CHILLING **MAKES:** 2 SERVINGS OR 3 CUPS

- 2 large oranges
- 1 large ripe tomato, cored and quartered
- 2 large stalks celery, peeled and sliced
- 1 cup ice cubes
- 1 teaspoon sugar

Into blender, squeeze juice from oranges. Add tomato, celery, ice, and sugar. Blend until smooth. Refrigerate until very cold. Pour into 2 tall glasses.

EACH SERVING: ABOUT 85 CALORIES, 2G PROTEIN, 19G CARBOHYDRATES, 1G TOTAL FAT (0G SATURATED), 0MG CHOLESTEROL, 55MG SODIUM.

Lean, Mean, and Green

Tarragon adds a note of surprise to this spinach and cucumber blend.

ACTIVE TIME: 5 MINUTES **TOTAL TIME:** 5 MINUTES **MAKES:** 2 SERVINGS OR 3 CUPS

- 1 package (10 ounces) frozen chopped spinach, broken up into chunks
- 2 medium Kirby cucumbers, peeled and sliced
- 2 cups apple juice
- 1 tablespoon fresh tarragon leaves

1 In blender, combine spinach, cucumbers, apple juice, and tarragon until smooth.

2 Strain through a fine sieve into a large measuring cup; discard pulp. Pour into 2 tall glasses.

EACH SERVING: ABOUT 165 CALORIES, 6G PROTEIN, 31G CARBOHYDRATES, 1G TOTAL FAT (0G SATURATED), 0MG CHOLESTEROL, 115MG SODIUM.

"Milk" and Honey

Make use of lingering celery in your fridge with this blender juice that mixes almond milk, cucumber, and grapes for a sip-worthy snack.

ACTIVE TIME: 5 MINUTES **TOTAL TIME:** 5 MINUTES **MAKES:** 2 SERVINGS OR 3 CUPS

- 1½ cups sweetened almond milk
- 1 medium Kirby cucumber, peeled and sliced
- 1 cup seedless green grapes
- 2 medium stalks celery, peeled and sliced
- 1 tablespoon honey

In blender, combine almond milk, cucumber, grapes, celery, and honey until smooth. Pour into 2 tall glasses.

EACH SERVING: ABOUT 145 CALORIES, 2G PROTEIN, 32G CARBOHYDRATES, 2G TOTAL FAT (0G SATURATED), 0MG CHOLESTEROL, 165MG SODIUM.

TIP

In place of unsweetened almond milk, other options can be used like soy milk, regular milk, almond milk, or even coconut milk.

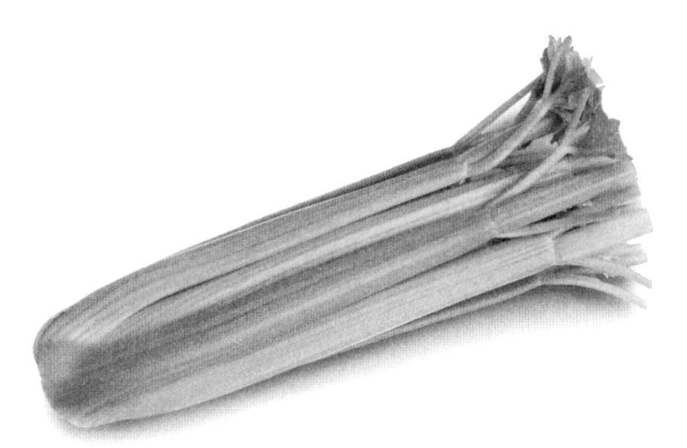

Beet Red REFRESHER

This red-hued juice is as delicious as it is gorgeous. A Granny Smith apple and drop of lemon juice add a touch of tartness.

ACTIVE TIME: 10 MINUTES **TOTAL TIME:** 10 MINUTES **MAKES:** 2 SERVINGS OR 3 CUPS

- 2 cups fresh strawberries (about 8 ounces), hulled and quartered
- 1½ cups cold water
- 1 cup sliced precooked beets (not canned; see tip)
- ½ small Granny Smith apple, peeled and thinly sliced
- 3 tablespoons fresh lemon juice
- 1 tablespoon agave nectar (see tip, page 46)

In blender, combine strawberries, water, beets, apple, lemon juice, and agave until smooth. Pour into 2 tall glasses.

EACH SERVING: ABOUT 120 CALORIES, 2G PROTEIN, 30G CARBOHYDRATES, 1G TOTAL FAT (0G SATURATED), 0MG CHOLESTEROL, 65MG SODIUM.

Beets are chockfull of nutrients with high levels of both magnesium and potassium. These ruby-red root vegetables also help aid in preventing cardiovascular diseases with betalain and protect against birth defects with folic acid.

Spring IN A GLASS

This is blushy pink perfection to cool you down on a warm day.

ACTIVE TIME: 10 MINUTES **TOTAL TIME:** 10 MINUTES **MAKES:** 2 SERVINGS OR 3½ CUPS

- 2 medium stalks rhubarb, sliced; or 1½ cups frozen chopped rhubarb
- 3 tablespoons sugar
- 1 container (6 ounces) fresh raspberries
- 1 cup cold water
- 1 cup ice cubes
- 1 small (½-inch) piece fresh peeled ginger, sliced (see tip)

1 In medium microwave-safe bowl, combine rhubarb and sugar. Microwave, uncovered, on High 2 minutes or until rhubarb falls apart. Let cool completely.

2 In blender, combine cooked rhubarb, raspberries, water, ice, and ginger until smooth. Pour into 2 tall glasses.

EACH SERVING: ABOUT 130 CALORIES, 2G PROTEIN, 32G CARBOHYDRATES, 1G TOTAL FAT (0G SATURATED), 0MG CHOLESTEROL, 5MG SODIUM.

Fresh ginger can also be chopped, sliced, or julienned with a sharp knife, box grater, or microplane before being added to recipes. To store fresh gingerroot in the refrigerator, wrap it in a paper towel, then tightly in plastic wrap. It will stay fresh for up to 2 weeks.

Pink Basil BLEND

An herbal lushness is added to this watermelon-based juice that harnesses summer no matter what season of the year.

ACTIVE TIME: 10 MINUTES **TOTAL TIME:** 10 MINUTES **MAKES:** 2 SERVINGS OR 2¼ CUPS

- 3 cups watermelon chunks
- 1 cup freshly grated, peeled carrot (see tip)
- ½ cup loosely packed fresh basil leaves
- 2 teaspoons fresh lemon juice
- pinch salt

In blender, combine watermelon, carrot, basil, lemon juice, and salt until smooth. Pour into 2 tall glasses.

EACH SERVING: ABOUT 85 CALORIES, 2G PROTEIN, 26G CARBOHYDRATES, 0G TOTAL FAT (0G SATURATED), 0MG CHOLESTEROL, 115MG SODIUM.

TIP

Sure, you know that carrots are rich in beta carotene. But were you aware that this compound reduces heart disease and also prevents some cancers? If you have a carrot or two in the fridge, it never hurts to throw it into the blender to be included in a smoothie or blender juice.

Banana Split Shake
(page 62)

4 Soda Fountain & Coffee Bar

Milkshakes and fountain drinks enchant kids and adults alike. Celebrate with the towering amazement of the Banana-Split Shake. Other delights include milkshakes in a variety of flavors like strawberry and chocolate, plus the nostalgia tastiness of malted milkshakes.

Usher in a wintery allure with the Peppermint Stick Shake or indulge the chocoholic in your life with the Peanut-Butter-Cup Shake. For a fruity approach, the Lemon-Berry Shake and Key Lime Shake offer tart refreshment. Floats include the well-known Root Beer Float and the fruity twist of our Passion Fruit Float. You'll soon be banishing store-bought frozen coffee concoctions after whipping up a Frosty Cappuccino or Mocha Frappa Cinno, a more delicious and affordable approach. Cap off any meal with the sweet, iced frothy delight of Frozen Hot Chocolate.

Double-Chocolate MALTED MILKSHAKE

Malt powder enriches the flavor of any milkshake. Look for it near the cocoa powder in your supermarket.

ACTIVE TIME: 5 MINUTES **TOTAL TIME:** 5 MINUTES **MAKES:** 2 SERVINGS OR 3 CUPS

- 4 scoops chocolate ice cream
- 1 cup milk
- 3 tablespoons chocolate syrup
- 3 tablespoons malted milk powder

In blender, combine ice cream, milk, chocolate syrup, and malt powder and blend until mixture is smooth and frothy. Pour into 2 tall glasses.

EACH SERVING: ABOUT 348 CALORIES, 9G PROTEIN, 47G CARBOHYDRATE, 13G TOTAL FAT (0G SATURATED), 44MG CHOLESTEROL, 153MG SODIUM.

Banana-Split SHAKE

Crown with whipped cream, chopped nuts, and maraschino cherries—then drizzle a little fudge sauce over the top. Photo on page 60.

ACTIVE TIME: 10 MINUTES **TOTAL TIME:** 10 MINUTES **MAKES:** 2 SERVINGS OR 2½ CUPS

- 4 tablespoons fudge sauce, plus more for garnish
- 1 banana, diced
- 4 mini scoops chocolate ice cream
- 4 mini scoops strawberry ice cream
- 4 scoops vanilla ice cream
- 1 cup milk
- whipped cream
- 1 tablespoon chopped walnuts or pecans
- 2 maraschino cherries

1 In each of 2 tall glasses, place 2 tablespoons fudge sauce, half of the diced banana, 2 mini scoops chocolate ice cream, and 2 mini scoops strawberry ice cream.

2 In blender, combine vanilla ice cream and milk and blend until mixture is smooth. Add mixture to glasses; top each with whipped cream, nuts, and a cherry and drizzle with fudge sauce.

EACH SERVING: ABOUT 537 CALORIES, 11G PROTEIN, 68G CARBOHYDRATE, 26G TOTAL FAT (14G SATURATED), 71MG CHOLESTEROL, 288MG SODIUM.

Double-Chocolate Malted Milkshake

Strawberry MALTED MILKSHAKE

If you like berry goodness, you'll love this malted. You'll find strawberry-flavored syrup with the other syrups and drink mixes in your supermarket.

ACTIVE TIME: 5 MINUTES **TOTAL TIME:** 5 MINUTES **MAKES:** 2 SERVINGS OR 2½ CUPS

- 4 scoops strawberry ice cream
- 1 cup milk
- 3 tablespoons malted milk powder
- 2 tablespoons strawberry-flavored syrup

In blender, combine ice cream, milk, malt powder, and strawberry syrup and blend until mixture is smooth and frothy. Pour into 2 tall glasses.

EACH SERVING: ABOUT 306 CALORIES, 8G PROTEIN, 44G CARBOHYDRATE, 11G TOTAL FAT (7G SATURATED), 39MG CHOLESTEROL, 130MG SODIUM.

Classic Vanilla MILKSHAKE

This is a truly singular sensation.

ACTIVE TIME: 5 MINUTES **TOTAL TIME:** 5 MINUTES **MAKES:** 2 SERVINGS OR 2½ CUPS

- 5 scoops vanilla ice cream
- 1 cup milk
- 1 teaspoon vanilla extract

In blender, combine ice cream, milk, and vanilla, and blend until mixture is smooth and frothy. Pour into 2 tall glasses.

EACH SERVING: ABOUT 269 CALORIES, 6G PROTEIN, 23G CARBOHYDRATE, 16G TOTAL FAT (10G SATURATED), 60MG CHOLESTEROL, 97MG SODIUM.

Classic Chocolate MILKSHAKE

For those who delight in all things from the cocoa bean, make this double helping—chocolate ice cream and chocolate syrup.

ACTIVE TIME: 5 MINUTES **TOTAL TIME:** 5 MINUTES **MAKES:** 2 SERVINGS OR 2¼ CUPS

- 4 scoops vanilla or chocolate ice cream
- ¾ cup milk
- ¼ cup chocolate syrup

In blender, combine ice cream, milk, and chocolate syrup and blend until mixture is smooth and frothy. Pour into 2 tall glasses.

EACH SERVING: ABOUT 311 CALORIES, 6G PROTEIN, 43G CARBOHYDRATE, 13G TOTAL FAT (8G SATURATED), 47MG CHOLESTEROL, 102MG SODIUM.

Mocha MALTED MILKSHAKE

The best of all possible worlds—coffee, chocolate, and malted milk all served up together in a tall glass.

ACTIVE TIME: 5 MINUTES **TOTAL TIME:** 5 MINUTES **MAKES:** 2 SERVINGS OR 2 CUPS

- 4 scoops coffee ice cream
- 1 cup milk
- 2 tablespoons chocolate syrup
- 2 tablespoons malted milk powder

In blender, combine ice cream, milk, chocolate syrup, and malt powder and blend until mixture is smooth and frothy. Pour into 2 tall glasses.

EACH SERVING: ABOUT 297 CALORIES, 7G PROTEIN, 39G CARBOHYDRATE, 13G TOTAL FAT (8G SATURATED), 43MG CHOLESTEROL, 137MG SODIUM.

Peppermint Stick Shake

Peppermint Stick SHAKE

Use candy-cane sticks as stirrers. Kids will love it.

ACTIVE TIME: 10 MINUTES **TOTAL TIME:** 10 MINUTES **MAKES:** 2 SERVINGS OR 2 CUPS

- 8 round hard peppermint candies
- 4 scoops vanilla ice cream
- ¾ cup milk
- ¼ teaspoon peppermint extract
- 2 peppermint sticks for garnish (optional)

In blender, blend candies until finely crushed. Add ice cream, milk, and peppermint extract and blend until mixture is smooth and frothy. Pour into 2 tall glasses. Garnish with peppermint sticks, if you like.

EACH SERVING: ABOUT 302 CALORIES, 5G PROTEIN, 42G CARBOHYDRATE, 13G TOTAL FAT (8G SATURATED), 47MG CHOLESTEROL, 84MG SODIUM.

Dulce de Leche SHAKE

Dulce de leche ice cream tastes even richer and more flavorful when paired with caramel sauce.

ACTIVE TIME: 5 MINUTES **TOTAL TIME:** 5 MINUTES **MAKES:** 2 SERVINGS OR 2½ CUPS

- 1 cup milk
- 4 scoops dulce de leche ice cream
- 2 tablespoons caramel sauce

In blender, combine milk, ice cream, and caramel sauce and blend until mixture is smooth and frothy. Pour into 2 tall glasses.

EACH SERVING: ABOUT 430 CALORIES, 9G PROTEIN, 49G CARBOHYDRATE, 21G TOTAL FAT (13G SATURATED), 117MG CHOLESTEROL, 225MG SODIUM.

Frosty CAPPUCCINO

Better than store-bought! A deceptively rich blender drink.

ACTIVE TIME: 5 MINUTES **TOTAL TIME:** 5 MINUTES **MAKES:** 2 SERVINGS OR 1½ CUPS

1 cup low-fat (1 percent) milk
1 tablespoon chocolate syrup
1 teaspoon instant espresso-coffee powder
2 ice cubes
sugar (optional)
⅛ teaspoon ground cinnamon for garnish

In blender, combine milk, chocolate syrup, espresso powder, and ice and blend until mixture is smooth and frothy. Add sugar to taste, if you like. Pour into 2 chilled glasses. Sprinkle with cinnamon.

EACH SERVING: ABOUT 75 CALORIES, 4G PROTEIN, 12G CARBOHYDRATE, 1G TOTAL FAT (1G SATURATED), 5MG CHOLESTEROL, 65MG SODIUM.

Mocha FRAPPA CINNO

Our version of that famous coffee bar favorite. You can make it at home in a flash.

ACTIVE TIME: 10 MINUTES **TOTAL TIME:** 10 MINUTES **MAKES:** 4 SERVINGS OR 4 CUPS

3 cups ice cubes
1 cup strong brewed coffee, chilled
¾ cup milk
⅓ cup fudge sauce
2 tablespoons sugar

In blender, combine ice, coffee, milk, fudge sauce, and sugar and blend until mixture is smooth and frothy. Pour into 4 glasses.

EACH SERVING: ABOUT 145 CALORIES, 3G PROTEIN, 24G CARBOHYDRATE, 4G TOTAL FAT (2G SATURATED), 6MG CHOLESTEROL, 63MG SODIUM.

Frosty Cappuccino

Creamy Orange SHAKE

Brings back memories of a favorite ice cream treat.

ACTIVE TIME: 5 MINUTES **TOTAL TIME:** 5 MINUTES **MAKES:** 2 SERVINGS OR 2½ CUPS

- 5 scoops vanilla ice cream
- ½ cup orange juice
- ⅓ cup milk
- ⅓ cup frozen orange juice concentrate
- orange peel for garnish (optional)

In blender, combine ice cream, orange juice, milk, and orange juice concentrate and blend until mixture is smooth and frothy. Pour into 2 tall glasses. Garnish with orange peel, if you like.

EACH SERVING: ABOUT 341 CALORIES, 5G PROTEIN, 43G CARBOHYDRATE, 14G TOTAL FAT (8G SATURATED), 49MG CHOLESTEROL, 59MG SODIUM.

Root Beer FLOAT

This wonderful combination goes back to great grandma's day. In the 1960s, root beer floats were served in big mugs at A&W drive-ins by car-hops and waitresses on roller skates.

ACTIVE TIME: 5 MINUTES **TOTAL TIME:** 5 MINUTES **MAKES:** 2 SERVINGS OR 3 CUPS

- 4 scoops vanilla ice cream
- 1 can (12 ounces) root beer, chilled

1 In blender, combine 2 scoops ice cream and ¾ cup root beer and blend until mixture is smooth. Pour into 2 tall glasses.

2 Add a scoop of ice cream to each glass and fill with remaining root beer.

EACH SERVING: ABOUT 226 CALORIES, 2G PROTEIN, 34G CARBOHYDRATE, 10G TOTAL FAT (6G SATURATED), 35MG CHOLESTEROL, 54MG SODIUM.

Lemon-Berry SHAKE

The sweetness of the berries is balanced by the tang of fresh lemon. Served in a tall glass, this shake looks as pretty as a parfait.

ACTIVE TIME: 15 MINUTES **TOTAL TIME:** 15 MINUTES **MAKES:** 2 SERVINGS OR 2⅔ CUPS

- 1 cup strawberries, hulled
- ¼ cup raspberries
- 2 tablespoons sugar
- 2 to 3 lemons
- 4 scoops vanilla ice cream
- ¾ cup milk

1 In blender, combine strawberries, raspberries, and sugar and blend until smooth. Pour into a glass; refrigerate.

2 From lemons, grate 1½ teaspoons peel and squeeze ⅓ cup juice.

3 In clean blender, combine lemon peel, lemon juice, ice cream, and milk and blend until mixture is smooth. Pour half of lemon mixture into 2 tall glasses. Top with half of berry puree. Repeat and gently stir until swirled.

EACH SERVING: ABOUT 293 CALORIES, 6G PROTEIN, 41G CARBOHYDRATE, 13G TOTAL FAT (8G SATURATED), 47MG CHOLESTEROL, 76MG SODIUM.

Peach Melba SHAKE

Here's a great new take on a timeless classic. We took the flavors that made peach melba such a popular dessert and used them to make this sensational shake.

ACTIVE TIME: 5 MINUTES **TOTAL TIME:** 5 MINUTES **MAKES:** 2 SERVINGS OR 2½ CUPS

- 2 scoops vanilla ice cream
- 3 canned peaches in heavy syrup, drained
- 1 drop almond extract
- 2 scoops raspberry sorbet
- ½ cup cranberry-raspberry juice cocktail, chilled

1 In blender, combine ice cream, peaches, and almond extract and blend until mixture is smooth. Pour into glass measuring cup.

2 In same blender, combine sorbet and juice and blend until mixture is smooth. Pour half the peach and raspberry mixtures simultaneously into a glass so the shake is half peach- and half raspberry-colored. Repeat with the remaining mixtures in another glass.

EACH SERVING: ABOUT 279 CALORIES, 2G PROTEIN, 60G CARBOHYDRATE, 5G TOTAL FAT (3G SATURATED), 18MG CHOLESTEROL, 35MG SODIUM.

Passion Fruit FLOAT

A sparkling taste of the tropics.

ACTIVE TIME: 5 MINUTES **TOTAL TIME:** 5 MINUTES **MAKES:** 2 SERVINGS OR 2½ CUPS

1 can (12 ounces) lemon-lime soda, chilled
2 scoops passion fruit sorbet
2 scoops lemon sorbet

1 In blender, combine ¾ cup soda and passion fruit sorbet and blend until mixture is smooth. Pour into 2 tall glasses.

2 Add a scoop of lemon sorbet to each glass. Fill with remaining soda.

EACH SERVING: ABOUT 202 CALORIES, 0G PROTEIN, 46G CARBOHYDRATE, 0G TOTAL FAT (0G SATURATED), 0MG CHOLESTEROL, 56MG SODIUM.

Key Lime SHAKE

Kick back while you enjoy this refreshing shake, reminiscent of the laid-back Florida keys.

ACTIVE TIME: 5 MINUTES **TOTAL TIME:** 5 MINUTES **MAKES:** 2 SERVINGS OR 3 CUPS

- 4 scoops vanilla ice cream
- 1 cup milk
- ½ cup frozen limeade concentrate
- 1 teaspoon freshly grated lime peel

In blender, combine ice cream, milk, limeade concentrate, and lime peel and blend until mixture is smooth and frothy. Pour into 2 tall glasses.

EACH SERVING: ABOUT 361 CALORIES, 6G PROTEIN, 56G CARBOHYDRATE, 14G TOTAL FAT (9G SATURATED), 52MG CHOLESTEROL, 89MG SODIUM.

Frozen HOT CHOCOLATE

This low-fat treat takes the lusciousness of hot chocolate, turning it into an icy chocolate dream.

ACTIVE TIME: 10 MINUTES **TOTAL TIME:** 10 MINUTES **MAKES:** 1 SERVING

- ¾ cup low-fat (1 percent) milk
- 1 tablespoon plus 1 teaspoon unsweetened cocoa powder
- ½ teaspoon no-calorie sweetener
- ⅛ teaspoon pure vanilla extract
- 4 large ice cubes
- 1 tablespoon light whipped cream

In blender, combine milk, cocoa powder, sweetener, and vanilla extract. Blend until cocoa dissolves, scraping container. Add ice cubes; blend well. Pour into cup; top with whipped cream. Serve immediately.

EACH SERVING: ABOUT 117 CALORIES, 8G PROTEIN, 14G CARBOHYDRATE, 5G TOTAL FAT (3G SATURATED), 17MG CHOLESTEROL, 85MG SODIUM.

Peanut-Butter-Cup SHAKE

Chocolate and PB lovers will both be pleased with this candy-inspired confection.

ACTIVE TIME: 10 MINUTES **TOTAL TIME:** 10 MINUTES **MAKES:** 2 SERVINGS OR 3 CUPS

- 4 peanut-butter-cup candies (3 ounces total)
- 4 scoops chocolate ice cream
- 1 cup milk
- ¼ cup peanut butter

1 Chop peanut butter cups.

2 In blender, combine ice cream, milk, and peanut butter and blend until mixture is smooth. Add candies and blend until combined. Pour into 2 tall glasses.

EACH SERVING: ABOUT 685 CALORIES, 21G PROTEIN, 54G CARBOHYDRATE, 44G TOTAL FAT (17G SATURATED), 45MG CHOLESTEROL, 40MG SODIUM.

Classic Vanilla MALTED MILKSHAKE

Give it one taste, and you'll see why this thick creamy treat has been a soda fountain favorite for years.

ACTIVE TIME: 5 MINUTES **TOTAL TIME:** 5 MINUTES **MAKES:** 2 SERVINGS OR 2½ CUPS

- 4 scoops vanilla ice cream
- 1 cup milk
- 2 tablespoons malted milk powder
- ½ teaspoon vanilla extract

In blender, combine ice cream, milk, malt powder, and vanilla, and blend until mixture is smooth and frothy. Pour into 2 tall glasses.

EACH SERVING: ABOUT 258 CALORIES, 7G PROTEIN, 25G CARBOHYDRATE, 15G TOTAL FAT (9G SATURATED), 0MG CHOLESTEROL, 118MG SODIUM.

Coconut-Mango SHAKE

This icy, tropical combo conjures up island breezes. Be sure to use light coconut milk.

ACTIVE TIME: 10 MINUTES **TOTAL TIME:** 10 MINUTES **MAKES:** 2 SERVINGS OR 2½ CUPS

- 1 lime
- 3 scoops mango sorbet
- 1 cup light coconut milk
- ¼ cup water

1 From lime, grate 1½ teaspoons peel and squeeze 2 tablespoons juice.

2 In blender, combine lime peel, lime juice, mango sorbet, coconut milk, and water. Blend until mixture is smooth and frothy. Pour shake into 2 tall glasses.

EACH SERVING: ABOUT 203 CALORIES, 2G PROTEIN, 30G CARBOHYDRATE, 10G TOTAL FAT (6G SATURATED), 0MG CHOLESTEROL, 15MG SODIUM.

Frozen Watermelon Slush

5 Frozen Cocktails & Slushes

Making frozen drinks at home is a cinch thanks to the blender. Add a Classic Bellini or nonalcoholic Baby Bellini to brunch offerings or wind down in the evening with a Strawberry Margarita or Frozen Pina Colada. Whip out pitchers of Pomegranate Margaritas or the nonalcoholic Frozen Iced Tea for party throwing.

Don't forget about slushy offerings. Red Wine Sangria Slush riffs on the popular fruit-spiked drink, and the Mint Julep Slush is begging to be sipped whether it's Kentucky Derby time or not. The Miami Mojito is a mint lover's dream and the pineapple- and rum-heavy Cool Blue Hawaii beckons the beach, even when you're not near one. Whatever your chilled drink needs are, this chapter delivers.

Classic DAIQUIRI

The quintessential cocktail. You'll need 2 to 3 limes to get ¼ cup juice.

ACTIVE TIME: 5 MINUTES **TOTAL TIME:** 5 MINUTES **MAKES:** 4 SERVINGS OR 3¾ CUPS

- 4 cups ice cubes
- ¾ cup light rum
- ¼ cup fresh lime juice
- ¼ cup simple syrup, chilled (opposite)

In blender, combine ice, rum, lime juice, and simple syrup and blend until mixture is smooth. Pour into 4 glasses.

EACH SERVING: ABOUT 146 CALORIES, 0G PROTEIN, 13G CARBOHYDRATE, 0G TOTAL FAT (0G SATURATED), 0MG CHOLESTEROL, 1MG SODIUM.

Banana DAIQUIRI

Fruit makes a wonderful addition to daiquiris, marrying well with the rum. We used banana here, but peach, melon, strawberry, apricot, or mango would also be tasty.

ACTIVE TIME: 5 MINUTES **TOTAL TIME:** 5 MINUTES **MAKES:** 4 SERVINGS OR 4 CUPS

- 3 cups ice cubes
- 3 small ripe bananas, cut into chunks (about 2 cups)
- ¾ cup light rum
- ¼ cup fresh lime juice (from 2 to 3 limes)
- 2 tablespoons simple syrup, chilled (opposite)

In blender, combine ice, bananas, rum, lime juice, and simple syrup and blend until mixture is smooth. Pour into 4 glasses.

EACH SERVING: ABOUT 193 CALORIES, 1G PROTEIN, 25G CARBOHYDRATE, 1G TOTAL FAT (0G SATURATED), 0MG CHOLESTEROL, 1MG SODIUM.

Simple SYRUP

This sugar syrup is great in cold drinks, such as iced tea, because it dissolves instantly. Keep some on hand in the refrigerator—it will last for up to a month.

ACTIVE TIME: 5 MINUTES **TOTAL TIME:** 15 MINUTES **MAKES:** 2 CUPS

- 2 cups sugar
- 1 cup water

In a small saucepan, combine sugar and water. Bring to a boil. Reduce heat to low; simmer 10 minutes. Cool and refrigerate until chilled.

PER TEASPOON: ABOUT 16 CALORIES, 0G PROTEIN, 2G CARBOHYDRATE, 0G TOTAL FAT (0G SATURATED), 0MG CHOLESTEROL, 0MG SODIUM.

Frozen PIÑA COLADA

This sweet tropical drink was popular at the legendary Trader Vic's restaurant in New York City.

ACTIVE TIME: 5 MINUTES **TOTAL TIME:** 5 MINUTES **MAKES:** 4 SERVINGS OR 4 CUPS

- 4 cups ice cubes
- ¾ cup pineapple juice, chilled
- ½ cup golden rum (see tip page 96)
- ½ cup cream of coconut

In blender, combine ice, juice, rum, and cream of coconut and blend until mixture is smooth and frothy. Pour into 4 glasses.

EACH SERVING: ABOUT 236 CALORIES, 0G PROTEIN, 28G CARBOHYDRATE, 5G TOTAL FAT (4G SATURATED), 0MG CHOLESTEROL, 16MG SODIUM.

Pomegranate MARGARITA

This is party perfection—a sensational twist on the margarita premixed by the pitcherful.

ACTIVE TIME: 5 MINUTES **TOTAL TIME:** 5 MINUTES **MAKES:** 8 SERVINGS

- 2 cups ice
- ¾ can frozen limeade concentrate, thawed
- 1½ cups gold tequila
- 1 cups pomegranate juice
- ½ cup triple sec
- 2 limes
- ½ cup fresh pomegranate seeds (from ½ pomegranate)

In blender, combine ice cubes, limeade until well blended. Add tequila, pomegranate juice, and triple sec and blend until smooth. Cut each lime crosswise into ¼-inch-thick wheels; cut a slit in each wheel, from center to edge. To serve, place a few pomegranate seeds in each glass; place a lime wheel on rim.

EACH SERVING: ABOUT 215 CALORIES, 4G PROTEIN, 47G CARBOHYDRATE, 6G TOTAL FAT (1G SATURATED), 28MG CHOLESTEROL, 165MG SODIUM.

Frosty Margarita

Frosty MARGARITA

Break out the salsa and chips.

ACTIVE TIME: 5 MINUTES **TOTAL TIME:** 5 MINUTES **MAKES:** 4 SERVINGS OR 4 CUPS

- 4 cups ice cubes
- ½ cup tequila
- ½ cup Cointreau (orange-flavored liquer)
- ¼ cup fresh lime juice (from 2 to 3 limes)

In blender, combine ice, tequila, Cointreau, and lime juice and blend until mixture is smooth. Pour into 4 glasses.

EACH SERVING: ABOUT 154 CALORIES, 0G PROTEIN, 10G CARBOHYDRATE, 0G TOTAL FAT (0G SATURATED), 0 MG CHOLESTEROL, 1MG SODIUM.

Strawberry MARGARITA

Pretty in pink—our fruity variation on the frosty classic.

ACTIVE TIME: 10 MINUTES **TOTAL TIME:** 10 MINUTES **MAKES:** 4 SERVINGS OR 5 CUPS

- 4 cups ice cubes
- 1 pint strawberries, hulled and halved
- ½ cup tequila
- ⅓ cup Cointreau (orange-flavored liqueur)
- ¼ cup fresh lime juice (from 2 to 3 limes)

In blender, combine ice, berries, tequila, Cointreau, and lime juice and blend until mixture is smooth. Pour into 4 glasses.

EACH SERVING: ABOUT 149 CALORIES, 1G PROTEIN, 12G CARBOHYDRATE, 0G TOTAL FAT (0G SATURATED), 0MG CHOLESTEROL, 1MG SODIUM.

Red Wine Sangria SLUSH

A real crowd-pleaser. For a party, triple or quadruple the ingredients and pour into a chilled pitcher.

ACTIVE TIME: 5 MINUTES **TOTAL TIME:** 5 MINUTES **MAKES:** 4 SERVINGS OR 3 CUPS

- 2 cups ice cubes
- ¾ cup frozen pitted sweet cherries
- 1 cup fruity red wine, chilled
- ½ cup frozen orange juice concentrate
- 1 tablespoon fresh lime juice

In blender, combine ice, cherries, wine, orange juice concentrate, and lime juice and blend until mixture is smooth. Pour into 4 glasses.

EACH SERVING: ABOUT 142 CALORIES, 2G PROTEIN, 26G CARBOHYDRATE, 0G TOTAL FAT (0G SATURATED), 0MG CHOLESTEROL, 5MG SODIUM.

Mint Julep SLUSH

These taste so good you'll want to give a Kentucky Derby party.

ACTIVE TIME: 5 MINUTES **TOTAL TIME:** 5 MINUTES **MAKES:** 4 SERVINGS OR 3½ CUPS

- 8 large sprigs fresh mint
- 4 cups ice cubes
- ¾ cup bourbon
- ¼ cup simple syrup, chilled (page 83)

1 Remove leaves from mint.

2 In blender, combine ice, bourbon, and simple syrup and blend until mixture is smooth. Add mint leaves; blend until leaves are coarsely chopped. Pour into 4 glasses.

EACH SERVING: ABOUT 152 CALORIES, 0G PROTEIN, 12G CARBOHYDRATE, 0G TOTAL FAT (0G SATURATED), 0MG CHOLESTEROL, 1MG SODIUM.

Frozen Watermelon SLUSH

A refreshing, colorful drink for those dog days of summer. If you have extra watermelon, freeze it for more slushes. Photo on page 80.

ACTIVE TIME: 5 MINUTES **TOTAL TIME:** 5 MINUTES **MAKES:** 4 SERVINGS OR 3½ CUPS

- 3 cups cubed seedless watermelon
- 1 cup frozen strawberries
- 2 scoops lemon sorbet
- ¼ cup pineapple juice, chilled
- 2 tablespoons fresh lime juice

In blender, combine watermelon, strawberries, sorbet, pineapple juice, and lime juice and blend until mixture is smooth. Pour into 4 glasses.

EACH SERVING: ABOUT 87 CALORIES, 1G PROTEIN, 22G CARBOHYDRATE, 0G TOTAL FAT (0G SATURATED), 0MG CHOLESTEROL, 7MG SODIUM.

Raspberry-Lemon SLUSH

A tasty something to sip for guests who don't want alcohol. Garnish each with a slice of lemon.

ACTIVE TIME: 5 MINUTES **TOTAL TIME:** 5 MINUTES **MAKES:** 4 SERVINGS OR 4 CUPS

- 1 package (10 ounces) frozen raspberries in syrup, thawed
- 3 cups ice cubes
- ½ cup fresh lemon juice (from 3 large lemons)
- ¼ cup simple syrup, chilled (page 83)

1 In blender, puree raspberries until smooth. Strain through a fine sieve; discard seeds.

2 In blender, combine raspberry puree, ice, lemon juice, and simple syrup and blend until mixture is smooth. Pour into 4 glasses.

EACH SERVING: ABOUT 171 CALORIES, 1G PROTEIN, 43G CARBOHYDRATE, 0G TOTAL FAT (0G SATURATED), 0MG CHOLESTEROL, 21MG SODIUM.

Cool BLUE HAWAIIAN

This turquoise drink is a favorite in the islands.

ACTIVE TIME: 5 MINUTES **TOTAL TIME:** 5 MINUTES **MAKES:** 4 SERVINGS OR 4½ CUPS

- 4 cups ice cubes
- 1 cup pineapple juice, chilled
- ½ cup blue curaçao
- ½ cup light rum
- ½ cup cream of coconut (see tip, page 84)
- 4 pineapple slices

In blender, combine ice, pineapple juice, blue curaçao, rum, and cream of coconut and blend until mixture is smooth. Pour into 4 glasses. Garnish with pineapple slices.

EACH SERVING: ABOUT 366 CALORIES, 1G PROTEIN, 51G CARBOHYDRATE, 5G TOTAL FAT (4G SATURATED), 0MG CHOLESTEROL, 19MG SODIUM.

FROZEN Virgin Mary

To make them more festive, garnish each drink with a lemon wedge. Then add a celery stalk to double as a stirrer.

ACTIVE TIME: 5 MINUTES **TOTAL TIME:** 5 MINUTES **MAKES:** 4 SERVINGS OR 4 CUPS

- 3 cups ice cubes
- 2 cups vegetable juice, chilled
- 3 tablespoons fresh lemon juice
- 1 to 2 teaspoons prepared white horseradish
- 1 teaspoon Worcestershire sauce
- ¼ to ½ teaspoon hot pepper sauce
- ⅛ teaspoon coarsely ground black pepper

In blender, combine ice, vegetable juice, lemon juice, horseradish, Worcestershire, hot pepper sauce, and black pepper and blend until smooth. Pour into 4 tall glasses.

EACH SERVING: ABOUT 30 CALORIES, 1G PROTEIN, 6G CARBOHYDRATE, 0G TOTAL FAT (0G SATURATED), 0MG CHOLESTEROL, 330MG SODIUM.

To turn this into a full-fledged Frozen Bloody Mary, pour 1 cup vodka into the blender with the ingredients and puree.

FROZEN **Iced Tea**

Lemon or passion fruit sorbet would also be delicious in this drink.

ACTIVE TIME: 5 MINUTES **TOTAL TIME:** 5 MINUTES **MAKES:** 4 SERVINGS OR 3½ CUPS

- 4 scoops orange sorbet
- 2 cups strong brewed black tea, at room temperature

In blender, combine sorbet and tea and blend until mixture is smooth. Pour into 4 glasses.

EACH SERVING: ABOUT 61 CALORIES, 0G PROTEIN, 15G CARBOHYDRATE, 0G TOTAL FAT (0G SATURATED), 0MG CHOLESTEROL, 11MG SODIUM.

MIAMI **Mojito**

This rum sparkler with its mint infusion is perfect for slow sipping while you watch a South Beach or, indeed, any sunset.

ACTIVE TIME: 10 MINUTES **TOTAL TIME:** 10 MINUTES **MAKES:** 6 SERVINGS OR 6 CUPS

- 8 large sprigs fresh mint, plus more for garnish
- ½ cup sugar
- ¼ cup fresh lime juice (from 2 to 3 limes)
- ½ teaspoon freshly grated lime peel
- 4 cups ice cubes
- 1 cup golden rum (see tip)
- 3 cups club soda

1 Remove leaves from mint sprigs. In blender, combine mint leaves, sugar, lime juice, and peel. Pulse until mint is chopped.

2 Fill pitcher with ice and add mint mixture. Pour in rum; stir. Fill with club soda. Pour into 6 glasses. Garnish with mint sprigs.

EACH SERVING: ABOUT 158 CALORIES, 0G PROTEIN, 17G CARBOHYDRATE, 0G TOTAL FAT (0G SATURATED), 0MG CHOLESTEROL, 26MG SODIUM.

TIP

Golden rums are also referred to as medium-bodied rums or amber runs. With a deep, almost caramel coloring, they are aged to around the three year mark and boast a more robust flavor than light rums.

BRANDIED Eggnog

We used ice cream as the base for this eggnog, making it even richer and more festive—ideal for the holidays.

ACTIVE TIME: 5 MINUTES **TOTAL TIME:** 5 MINUTES **MAKES:** 4 SERVINGS OR 2¼ CUPS

- 5 scoops French vanilla ice cream
- ⅓ cup brandy
- ¼ cup milk
- 2 tablespoons Grand Marnier (orange-flavored liqueur)
- ¼ teaspoon grated nutmeg

In blender, combine ice cream, brandy, milk, Grand Marnier, and ⅛ teaspoon nutmeg and blend until mixture is smooth and frothy. Pour into 4 glasses and sprinkle with remaining ⅛ teaspoon nutmeg.

EACH SERVING: ABOUT 179 CALORIES, 2G PROTEIN, 13G CARBOHYDRATE, 7G TOTAL FAT (4G SATURATED), 36MG CHOLESTEROL, 26MG SODIUM.

FROZEN Whiskey Sour

A cool twist on the straight-up classic drink.

ACTIVE TIME: 5 MINUTES **TOTAL TIME:** 5 MINUTES **MAKES:** 4 SERVINGS OR 3½ CUPS

- 4 cups ice cubes
- 1 can (6 ounces) frozen lemonade concentrate
- ¾ cup whiskey

In blender, combine ice, lemonade concentrate, and whiskey and blend until mixture is smooth. Pour into 4 glasses.

EACH SERVING: ABOUT 209 CALORIES, 0G PROTEIN, 26G CARBOHYDRATE, 0G TOTAL FAT (0G SATURATED), 0MG CHOLESTEROL, 3MG SODIUM.

Classic Bellini

The original, created at Harry's Bar in Venice, was white peaches. Look for them in June and July in the produce section of your market.

ACTIVE TIME: 5 MINUTES **TOTAL TIME:** 5 MINUTES **MAKES:** 4 SERVINGS OR 4 CUPS

- 2 ripe white or yellow peaches, pitted and diced
- 2 teaspoons fresh lemon juice
- 2 teaspoons simple syrup, chilled (page 83)
- 1 bottle (750 ml) Brut champagne or sparkling wine, chilled

In blender, combine peaches, lemon juice, and simple syrup and blend until mixture is smooth. Pour into 4 champagne flutes, then fill with champagne.

EACH SERVING: ABOUT 162 CALORIES, 1G PROTEIN, 12G CARBOHYDRATE, 0G TOTAL FAT (0G SATURATED), 0MG CHOLESTEROL, 0MG SODIUM.

Baby Bellini

Our nonalcoholic Bellini, made with sparkling apple juice, stays as bubbly as the original.

ACTIVE TIME: 5 MINUTES **TOTAL TIME:** 5 MINUTES **MAKES:** 4 SERVINGS OR 4 CUPS

- 2 ripe peaches, pitted and diced
- 2 teaspoons fresh lemon juice
- 2 teaspoons simple syrup, chilled (page 83)
- 1 bottle (750 ml) sparkling apple juice, chilled

In blender, combine peaches, lemon juice, and simple syrup and blend until mixture is smooth. Pour into 4 champagne flutes, then fill with sparkling apple juice.

EACH SERVING: ABOUT 122 CALORIES, 0G PROTEIN, 30G CARBOHYDRATE, 0G TOTAL FAT (0G SATURATED), 0MG CHOLESTEROL, 6MG SODIUM.

Irish Frost

A mocha-flavored milkshake—for adults only.

ACTIVE TIME: 5 MINUTES **TOTAL TIME:** 5 MINUTES **MAKES:** 5 SERVINGS OR 2¾ CUPS

- 5 scoops vanilla ice cream
- ¼ cup Bailey's Irish Cream
- ¼ cup white crème de cacao
- ¼ cup Kahlúa (coffee-flavored liqueur)
- ¼ cup milk
- 2 tablespoons vodka

In blender, combine ice cream, Bailey's, crème de cacao, Kahlúa, milk, and vodka and blend until mixture is smooth and frothy. Pour into 5 glasses.

EACH SERVING: ABOUT 221 CALORIES, 2G PROTEIN, 20G CARBOHYDRATE, 7G TOTAL FAT (5G SATURATED), 21MG CHOLESTEROL, 34MG SODIUM.

CREAMY Grasshopper

This is an ultra-rich, chilled variation on the original. With a crisp cookie, it makes a great dessert.

ACTIVE TIME: 5 MINUTES **TOTAL TIME:** 5 MINUTES **MAKES:** 4 SERVINGS OR 2¼ CUPS

- 4 scoops vanilla ice cream
- ⅓ cup green crème de menthe
- ⅓ cup white crème de cacao
- ⅓ cup milk

In blender, combine ice cream, crème de menthe, crème de cacao, and milk. Blend until mixture is smooth and frothy. Pour into 4 glasses.

EACH SERVING: ABOUT 254 CALORIES, 2G PROTEIN, 27G CARBOHYDRATE, 6G TOTAL FAT (3G SATURATED), 20MG CHOLESTEROL, 27MG SODIUM.

New England Clam Chowder
(page 108)

6 Soups, Dressings & Dips

Smoothies and drinks aren't the only recipes to be buzzed in your blender. It's the perfect vehicle for creamy vegetable-based soups like Quick Cream of Broccoli or Minted Pea Soup. Treat your family to the vibrant Tomato Soup, served alongside grilled cheese halves for dipping. Turn beans silky in the Spiced Lentil Soup or the Black Bean Dip.

Conquer potlucks and party appetizers with a selection of slather-worthy dips. The Roasted Red Pepper and Walnut Dip is primed and ready for pita triangles and the lime-enhanced Peanut-Coconut Dip offers a touch of exoticness to any dipping needs. Indulge in the deliciousness of homemade dressings like Ranch and Caesar—and they're almost as easy as the bottled variety. Easy directions in the *Good Housekeeping* style make Hollandaise Sauce approachable, just begging to be slathered over vegetables or Eggs Benedict.

Roasted Carrot SOUP

The sweetness of the caramelized carrots gels added zip from ginger and fresh herbs in this creamy soup.

ACTIVE TIME: 35 MINUTES **TOTAL TIME:** 1 HOUR **MAKES:** 8 APPETIZER SERVINGS

- 3 pounds carrots, cut into 1-inch chunks
- 1 tablespoon olive oil
- ⅛ teaspoon cayenne (ground red) pepper
- 1 teaspoon salt
- 2 tablespoons margarine or butter
- 2 medium shallots, chopped
- 3 cloves garlic, chopped
- 2 teaspoons fresh thyme leaves
- 4 cups chicken or vegetable broth
- 3 cups carrot juice
- 1 piece (1-inch) peeled fresh ginger (see tip, page 45), thinly sliced
- ¼ cup plain, nonfat Greek yogurt for garnish

chives for garnish

1 Preheat oven to 475°F. On large jelly-roll pan, toss carrots with oil, cayenne pepper, and ¼ teaspoon salt. Spread carrots in single layer and roast 30 to 35 minutes, or until carrots are caramelized, stirring once halfway through.

2 Meanwhile, in 5-quart sauce pot, melt margarine on medium heat. Add shallots, garlic, thyme, and ¼ teaspoon salt. Cook 3 minutes or until shallots are golden, stirring occasionally. Add roasted carrots, broth, juice, ginger, and remaining ½ teaspoon salt. Cover and heat to simmering on medium-high. Reduce heat to maintain simmer and cook, partially covered, 10 minutes or until carrots are tender.

3 With blender, puree mixture until smooth. Soup can be made and refrigerated up to 1 day ahead. Reheat on medium. To serve, top soup with yogurt and chives.

EACH SERVING: ABOUT 150 CALORIES, 3G PROTEIN, 25G CARBOHYDRATE, 5G TOTAL FAT (2G SATURATED), 10MG CHOLESTEROL, 960MG SODIUM.

Quick Cream of Broccoli SOUP

Frozen vegetables are picked and processed so quickly they often retain more nutrients than fresh. Here, broccoli and our other variations easily transform into satisfying soups.

ACTIVE TIME: 5 MINUTES **TOTAL TIME:** 25 MINUTES **MAKES:** 4 FIRST-COURSE SERVINGS OR 3¾ CUPS

1 tablespoon butter or margarine
1 medium onion, chopped
1 package (10 ounces) frozen chopped broccoli
1 can (14 ounces) chicken broth
¼ teaspoon dried thyme
⅛ teaspoon salt
⅛ teaspoon coarsely ground black pepper
Pinch ground nutmeg
Pinch cayenne (ground red) pepper, optional
1½ cups milk
2 teaspoons fresh lemon juice

1 In 3-quart saucepan, melt butter over medium heat. Add onion and cook, stirring occasionally, until tender, about 5 minutes. Add broccoli, broth, thyme, salt, pepper, nutmeg, and cayenne, if using; heat to boiling over high heat. Reduce heat and simmer 10 minutes.

2 In blender, with center part of cover removed to allow steam to escape, puree half of broccoli mixture until smooth. Pour pureed soup into large bowl after each batch. Repeat with remaining mixture.

3 Return puree to saucepan; stir in milk. Heat through, stirring often (do not boil). Remove from heat and stir in lemon juice.

EACH SERVING: ABOUT 130 CALORIES, 6G PROTEIN, 12G CARBOHYDRATE, 7G TOTAL FAT (4G SATURATED), 21MG CHOLESTEROL, 594MG SODIUM.

TIP

This Quick Cream of Broccoli soup is a base for any vegetable soup. Use a 10-ounce package of any frozen vegetable in place of the broccoli, like the options opposite or whatever catches your eye in the freezer section—such as peas, carrots, or spinach.

Variations

QUICK CREAM OF ASPARAGUS SOUP

Prepare as directed but substitute **1 package (10 ounces) frozen asparagus** for broccoli; if you like, add **¼ teaspoon dried tarragon** with broth.

QUICK CREAM OF SQUASH SOUP

Prepare as directed but substitute **1 package (10 ounces) frozen cooked winter squash** for broccoli; if you like, add **¼ teaspoon pumpkin-pie spice** after cooking onion and cook 30 seconds before adding broth.

QUICK CREAM OF CORN SOUP

Prepare as directed but substitute **1 package (10 ounces) frozen whole-kernel corn** for broccoli; if you like, add **¾ teaspoon chili powder** after cooking onion and cook 30 seconds before adding broth.

QUICK CREAM OF CAULIFLOWER SOUP

Prepare as directed but substitute **1 package (10 ounces) frozen cauliflower flowerets** for broccoli; if you like, add **½ teaspoon curry powder** after cooking onion and cook 30 seconds before adding broth. Garnish with **chopped fresh apple**.

Winter Vegetable SOUP

An elegant pureed soup that's perfect as a first course or, for a family dinner, just add salad, bread, and cheese.

ACTIVE TIME: 20 MINUTES **TOTAL TIME:** 50 MINUTES **MAKES:** 8 FIRST-COURSE SERVINGS OR 10 CUPS

1 tablespoon vegetable oil
1 medium onion, finely chopped
1 garlic clove, minced
1 bag (16 ounces) carrots, sliced
1 small fennel bulb, trimmed and diced
2 cans (14½ ounces each) chicken or vegetable broth
¼ teaspoon salt, or to taste
¼ teaspoon coarsely ground black pepper
3 cups water
3 medium all-purpose potatoes (about 1 pound), peeled and each cut into quarters
½ cup half-and-half or light cream (optional)
dill sprigs for garnish

1 In 5-quart saucepot, heat oil over medium heat. Add onion and garlic and cook 10 minutes or until tender, stirring occasionally. Stir in carrots, fennel, broth, salt, pepper, and water. Heat to boiling over high heat. Reduce heat to low; cover and simmer 10 minutes. Add potatoes and simmer 20 minutes longer or until vegetables are very tender.

2 In blender at low speed, with center part of cover removed to allow steam to escape, blend vegetable mixture in small batches until smooth; pour pureed soup into large bowl after each batch.

3 Return puree to saucepot; add half-and-half or light cream, if desired; heat through. Garnish each serving with a dill sprig.

EACH SERVING WITHOUT CREAM: ABOUT 100 CALORIES, 4G PROTEIN, 16G CARBOHYDRATE, 3G TOTAL FAT (0G SATURATED), 0MG CHOLESTEROL, 420MG SODIUM.

Spiced Lentil SOUP

Based on an Indian classic Mulligatawny, this thick and hearty soup is bound to become a staple in your repertoire. Lentils, unlike other dried legumes, don't require presoaking, so this can be prepared in less time than most bean soups.

ACTIVE TIME: 30 MINUTES **TOTAL TIME:** 1 HOUR, 40 MINUTES
MAKES: 5 MAIN-DISH SERVINGS OR 11 CUPS

2 tablespoons olive oil
4 carrots, peeled and finely chopped
2 large stalks celery, finely chopped
1 large onion (12 ounces), finely chopped
1 medium Granny Smith apple, peeled, cored, and finely chopped
1 tablespoon grated, peeled fresh ginger (see tip, page 45)
1 garlic clove, crushed with garlic press
2 teaspoons curry powder
¾ teaspoon ground cumin
¾ teaspoon ground coriander
1 package (16 ounces) lentils, rinsed and picked through
5 cups water
2 cans (14 ½ ounces each) vegetable or chicken broth
¼ cup chopped fresh cilantro
½ teaspoon salt
plain low-fat yogurt

1 In 5-quart Dutch oven, heat oil over medium-high heat. Add carrots, celery, onion, and apple; cook, stirring occasionally, until lightly browned, 10 to 15 minutes.

2 Add ginger, garlic, curry powder, cumin, and coriander; cook, stirring, 1 minute.

3 Add lentils, water, and broth; heat to boiling over high heat. Reduce heat; cover and simmer, stirring occasionally, until lentils are tender, 45 to 55 minutes.

4 In blender, with center part of cover removed to allow steam to escape, blend 5 cups soup in batches. Pour pureed soup into large bowl. Return soup to Dutch oven. Heat through. Stir in cilantro and salt. Ladle soup into 5 soup bowls; top each with a dollop of yogurt.

EACH SERVING: ABOUT 441 CALORIES, 29G PROTEIN, 71G CARBOHYDRATE, 8G TOTAL FAT (1G SATURATED), 0MG CHOLESTEROL, 963MG SODIUM.

Minted Pea SOUP

Fresh mint and sweet spring peas are a tried-and-true combo that's sure to impress.

ACTIVE TIME: 20 MINUTES **TOTAL TIME:** 1 HOUR 10 MINUTES **MAKES:** 8 FIRST-COURSE SERVINGS

- 2 tablespoons margarine or butter
- 1 tablespoon vegetable oil
- 1 medium (8 ounce) onion, chopped
- 2 garlic cloves, chopped
- ¼ teaspoon freshly grated nutmeg
- ¾ tablespoon salt
- 2 pounds shelled fresh (or thawed frozen) peas
- 1 quart low-sodium chicken broth
- 1 tablespoon chopped fresh mint leaves
- ¼ teaspoon coarsely ground black pepper
- ½ cup half-and-half
- 8 nasturtium flowers for garnish

1 In 7- to 8-quart saucepot, heat margarine and oil on medium, until margarine has melted. Add onion; cook 3 minutes, stirring occasionally. Add garlic, nutmeg, and ½ teaspoon salt. Cook 3 to 5 minutes or until onion has softened, stirring occasionally.

2 To same pot, add peas and broth. Heat to simmering on medium-high. Reduce heat to maintain simmer. Simmer 30 minutes or until peas are tender, stirring occasionally.

3 Add mint to soup. In blender or with immersion blender, puree until smooth. Stir in half-and-half and ¼ teaspoon each salt and pepper. If making ahead, cool and refrigerate in airtight container up to 2 days. (Soup may thicken; if so, thin with additional broth or water until desired consistency.) Reheat on medium until hot. Divide among serving bowls. Garnish with flowers.

EACH SERVING: ABOUT 165 CALORIES, 7G PROTEIN, 20G CARBOHYDRATE, 7G TOTAL FAT (2G SATURATED), 6MG CHOLESTEROL, 480MG SODIUM.

New England Clam CHOWDER

Classic and comforting, a bowl of creamy seafood soup is sure to please.
Photo on page 100.

ACTIVE TIME: 25 MINUTES **TOTAL TIME:** 45 MINUTES **MAKES:** 4 SERVINGS

- 2 tablespoons extra-virgin olive oil
- 1 medium onion, coarsely chopped
- 2 stalks celery, coarsely chopped
- 1 large russet potato, peeled and cut into ½-inch chunks
- 1 quart low-sodium chicken broth
- 2 bottles (8 ounces each) clam juice
- 2 cups corn kernels
- 1 teaspoon fresh thyme leaves, plus sprigs for garnish
- ¼ teaspoon smoked paprika
- ¼ teaspoon coarsely ground black pepper
- 12 ounces deveined shrimp, shelled, coarsely chopped
- 1 cup reduced-fat (2%) milk
- 2 medium tomatoes, seeded and finely chopped
- 4 whole-grain dinner rolls

1 In 6-quart saucepot, heat oil on medium. Add onion, celery, and potato. Cook 5 minutes, stirring. Add broth and clam juice. Heat to boiling on high. Cover partially; boil 10 to 15 minutes or until potato is very tender, stirring often.

2 In blender, puree mixture in batches until smooth. Add corn, thyme, paprika, and pepper. Heat to simmering on medium. Simmer 5 minutes, stirring.

3 To pot, add shrimp and milk. Cook 3 to 5 minutes or until shrimp just turn opaque, stirring occasionally. Divide chowder among 4 bowls. Top each with tomato; garnish with thyme springs. Serve with whole-grain rolls.

EACH SERVING: ABOUT 425 CALORIES, 23G PROTEIN, 60G CARBOHYDRATE, 12G TOTAL FAT (2G SATURATED), 116MG CHOLESTEROL, 1,440MG SODIUM.

Tomato SOUP

A sensational way to use up every last ripe summer tomato when flavor will be at its peak. For a creamier version, stir in heavy or light cream or plain yogurt to taste.

ACTIVE TIME: 20 MINUTES **TOTAL TIME:** 1 HOUR 30 MINUTES
MAKES: 8 FIRST-COURSE SERVINGS OR 8 CUPS

1 tablespoon butter or margarine
1 medium onion, diced
1 medium stalk celery, diced
1 medium carrot, peeled and diced
1 garlic clove, crushed with garlic press
2 teaspoons fresh thyme leaves
4 pounds ripe tomatoes, cut up
1 can (14½ ounces) chicken broth
¾ teaspoon salt
¼ teaspoon coarsely ground black pepper
1 bay leaf
½ cup water
snipped chives for garnish

1 In 5-quart Dutch oven, melt butter over low heat. Add onion, celery, and carrot; cook 10 minutes, until tender. Stir in garlic and thyme; cook 1 minute.

2 Add tomatoes, broth, salt, pepper, bay leaf, and water; heat to boiling over high heat. Reduce heat to medium-low and cook, uncovered, 45 minutes or until tomatoes are broken up and mixture has thickened slightly. Discard bay leaf.

3 In blender, with center part of cover removed to allow steam to escape, blend tomato mixture in small batches until pureed. Pour pureed soup into large bowl after each batch. Repeat with remaining mixture.

4 Refrigerate soup to serve cold. Or reheat soup in same Dutch oven to serve hot. Sprinkle with chives to serve.

EACH SERVING: ABOUT 80 CALORIES, 3G PROTEIN, 13G CARBOHYDRATE, 3G TOTAL FAT (1G SATURATED), 0MG CHOLESTEROL, 410MG SODIUM.

TIP

Craving tomato soup when tomatoes aren't at their peak? No problem. Just substitute two 28-ounce cans whole peeled tomatoes with their juices.

Peanut-Coconut DIP

This dip requires only a quick spin in a blender to prepare, but the Thai-inspired combination of flavors will wow your guests.

ACTIVE TIME: 5 MINUTES **TOTAL TIME:** 5 MINUTES **MAKES:** 1 CUP

1 cup peanuts
¼ cup coconut milk
2 tablespoons fresh lime juice
1 tablespoon lower-sodium soy sauce
1 tablespoon chopped shallot
2 tablespoons water
⅛ teaspoon salt
⅛ teaspoon coarsely ground black pepper
crudités, for serving (see tip)

In blender, combine peanuts, coconut milk, lime juice, soy sauce, shallot, water, salt, and pepper and blend until smooth. Serve with crudités.

EACH TABLESPOON: ABOUT 62 CALORIES, 2G PROTEIN, 2G CARBOHYDRATE, 5G TOTAL FAT (1G SATURATED), 0MG CHOLESTEROL, 54MG SODIUM.

The sky is the limit when it comes to assembling a crudité platter. Think strips of red bell peppers, asparagus spears, broccoli or cauliflower flowerets, fennel slices, sugar snap peas, radishes, cucumber rounds, and baby carrots.

Black Bean DIP

Mix and match white- and blue-corn tortilla chips to serve with this spicy Tex-Mex dip. You can substitute canned pinto beans or whatever beans you have in your pantry.

ACTIVE TIME: 5 MINUTES **TOTAL TIME:** 10 MINUTES **MAKES:** 2 CUPS

- 4 garlic cloves, peeled
- 1 can (15 to 19 ounces) black beans, rinsed and drained
- 2 tablespoons tomato paste
- 2 tablespoons olive oil
- 5 teaspoons fresh lime juice
- ½ teaspoon ground cumin
- ½ teaspoon ground coriander
- ¼ teaspoon salt
- ⅛ teaspoon cayenne (ground red) pepper

1 In 1-quart saucepan, place garlic and enough water to cover; heat to boiling over high heat. Reduce heat to low; cover and simmer 3 minutes to blanch garlic. Reserve *¾ cup blanching water.* Drain garlic.

2 In blender, combine *½ cup reserved water* and garlic; blend until smooth. Add beans, tomato paste, oil, lime juice, cumin, coriander, salt, and cayenne. Blend until smooth, adding remaining *¼ cup reserved water* if necessary, until mixture reaches dipping consistency. Spoon dip into bowl; cover and refrigerate up to 2 days.

EACH TABLESPOON: ABOUT 18 CALORIES, 1G PROTEIN, 3G CARBOHYDRATE, 1G TOTAL FAT (0G SATURATED), 0MG CHOLESTEROL, 54MG SODIUM.

Roasted Red Pepper and Walnut DIP

This delicious Middle Eastern dip is a perfect blend of sweetness and tang.

ACTIVE TIME: 30 MINUTES **TOTAL TIME:** 40 MINUTES, PLUS COOLING **MAKES:** 1½ CUPS

- 4 medium red peppers
- ½ cup walnuts
- ½ teaspoon ground cumin
- 2 slices firm white bread, torn into pieces
- 2 tablespoons raspberry or balsamic vinegar
- 1 tablespoon olive oil
- ½ teaspoon salt
- ⅛ teaspoon cayenne (ground red) pepper
- toasted pita triangles for serving

1 Line broiling pan with foil. Broil peppers at closest position to source of heat, turning occasionally, 10 minutes or until charred and blistered all over. Remove from broiler. Wrap foil around peppers and allow to steam at room temperature 15 minutes or until cool enough to handle.

2 Meanwhile, adjust oven control to 350°F. Spread walnuts in metal baking pan and bake 8 to 10 minutes, until toasted. In dry 1-quart saucepan, toast cumin over low heat 1 to 2 minutes, until very fragrant.

3 Remove peppers from foil. Peel off skin; discard skin and seeds. Cut peppers into large pieces. In blender, blend walnuts until ground. Add roasted peppers, cumin, bread, vinegar, olive oil, salt, and cayenne; blend until smooth, frequently stirring or scraping with spatula. Transfer to bowl. Cover and refrigerate if not serving right away. Remove from refrigerator 30 minutes before serving. Serve with toasted pita triangles.

EACH TABLESPOON: ABOUT 25 CALORIES, 0G PROTEIN, 2G CARBOHYDRATE, 2G TOTAL FAT (0G SATURATED), 0MG CHOLESTEROL, 40MG SODIUM.

Caesar Salad DRESSING

Just toss the dressing with crisp romaine lettuce leaves and toasted croutons, and you have a classic Caesar salad. Make it a main dish by adding grilled chicken or shrimp.

ACTIVE TIME: 10 MINUTES **TOTAL TIME:** 10 MINUTES **MAKES:** ¾ CUP

- 2 ounces Parmesan cheese, cut into small chunks
- 1 large garlic clove, peeled
- ¼ cup mayonnaise
- 3 tablespoons fresh lemon juice
- 3 tablespoons olive oil
- 2 tablespoons water
- 1 tablespoon Dijon mustard
- 2 teaspoons anchovy paste
- 1 teaspoon Worcestershire sauce
- ⅛ teaspoon coarsely ground black pepper

1 In blender, combine Parmesan cheese and garlic. Blend until cheese is finely grated.

2 Add mayonnaise, lemon juice, olive oil, water, mustard, anchovy paste, Worcestershire, and pepper and blend until combined. Transfer dressing to bowl or jar. Refrigerate at least 1 hour to allow flavors to blend.

EACH TABLESPOON: ABOUT 89 CALORIES, 2G PROTEIN, 1G CARBOHYDRATE, 9G TOTAL FAT (2G SATURATED), 7MG CHOLESTEROL, 150MG SODIUM.

Classic French VINAIGRETTE

Why use bottled dressings when it is so quick and easy to whip up a fresh homemade one in just minutes?

ACTIVE TIME: 5 MINUTES **TOTAL TIME:** 5 MINUTES **MAKES:** ¾ CUP

- ¼ cup red wine vinegar
- 1 tablespoon Dijon mustard
- ¾ teaspoon salt
- ½ teaspoon coarsely ground black pepper
- ½ cup olive oil

In blender, combine vinegar, mustard, salt, and pepper and blend until combined. Remove center of cover and, at low speed, very slowly pour in oil in steady stream, blending until mixed. Transfer to jar; cover and refrigerate up to 1 week.

EACH TABLESPOON: ABOUT 83 CALORIES, 0G PROTEIN, 0G CARBOHYDRATE, 9G TOTAL FAT (1G SATURATED), 0MG CHOLESTEROL, 153MG SODIUM.

Variations

MUSTARD-SHALLOT VINAIGRETTE

Prepare as directed but add **1 tablespoon minced shallot**. Cover and refrigerate up to 1 day. (Makes about ¾ cup.)

BLUE CHEESE VINAIGRETTE

Prepare as directed but add **2 ounces blue cheese, crumbled** (**½ cup**). Cover and refrigerate dressing up to 2 days. (Makes about 1 cup.)

Poppy Seed DRESSING

In the mood for a sweet-and-sour dressing? Spoon this gem over iceberg lettuce wedges or a colorful fresh fruit salad.

ACTIVE TIME: 10 MINUTES **TOTAL TIME:** 10 MINUTES **MAKES:** 1½ CUPS

- 1 cup vegetable oil
- ⅓ cup apple cider vinegar
- ½ cup sugar
- 1 tablespoon grated onion
- 1 tablespoon poppy seeds
- 1 teaspoon dry mustard
- 1 teaspoon salt

In blender, combine oil, vinegar, sugar, onion, poppy seeds, dry mustard, and salt and puree until smooth and thick. Transfer to jar; cover and refrigerate up to 2 days. Stir well before using.

EACH TABLESPOON: ABOUT 99 CALORIES, 0G PROTEIN, 4G CARBOHYDRATE, 9G TOTAL FAT (1G SATURATED), 0MG CHOLESTEROL, 97MG SODIUM.

Ranch DRESSING

Buttermilk gives Ranch Dressing its characteristic tang and creaminess. Use the large holes on a box grater to grate the onion.

ACTIVE TIME: 10 MINUTES **TOTAL TIME:** 10 MINUTES **MAKES:** ¾ CUP

- ½ cup buttermilk
- ⅓ cup mayonnaise
- 2 tablespoons fresh parsley leaves
- ½ teaspoon grated onion
- ¼ teaspoon salt
- ¼ teaspoon coarsely ground black pepper
- 1 garlic clove, cut in half

In blender, combine buttermilk, mayonnaise, parsley, onion, salt, and pepper and puree just until blended. Stir in garlic. Transfer to jar; cover and refrigerate up to 3 days. Remove garlic before serving.

EACH TABLESPOON: ABOUT 48 CALORIES, 0G PROTEIN, 1G CARBOHYDRATE, 5G TOTAL FAT (0G SATURATED), 1MG CHOLESTEROL, 93MG SODIUM.

Hollandaise SAUCE

Making a hollandaise has always seemed difficult because it is an emulsion that can break down if not heated properly. But making it in the blender actually helps stabilize the sauce. Delicious served with fish, vegetables, and that all-time favorite—Eggs Benedict.

ACTIVE TIME: 5 MINUTES **TOTAL TIME:** 5 MINUTES **MAKES:** 1 CUP

- 3 large egg yolks
- ¼ cup water
- 2 tablespoons fresh lemon juice
- ¼ teaspoon salt
- ½ cup butter (1 stick), melted (do not use margarine)

1 In heavy nonreactive 1-quart saucepan, with whisk, mix egg yolks, water, lemon juice, and salt until well blended. Cook over medium-low heat, stirring constantly with wooden spoon or heat-safe rubber spatula, until egg-yolk mixture just begins to bubble at edge, 6 to 8 minutes.

2 If necessary, reheat butter until hot. Pour yolk mixture into blender. With blender running at low speed and center of cover removed, add butter in a thin stream, blending until sauce is smooth and slightly thickened. If necessary, return sauce to saucepan, stirring constantly over low heat until hot.

EACH TABLESPOON: ABOUT 65 CALORIES, 1G PROTEIN, 0G CARBOHYDRATE, 7G TOTAL FAT (4G SATURATED), 56MG CHOLESTEROL, 100MG SODIUM.

Pesto

A dollop of this versatile sauce adds so much flavor to soups, such as minestrone or Tomato Soup (page 111). You can also toss it with cooked potatoes or pasta and even use it as a topping for pizza. Pesto freezes well, so you could make up several batches at once, to have on hand when fresh basil is out of season.

ACTIVE TIME: 10 MINUTES **TOTAL TIME:** 10 MINUTES **MAKES:** 1 CUP

- 1½ cups packed fresh basil leaves
- ½ cup freshly grated Parmesan cheese
- ⅓ cup olive oil
- ½ teaspoon salt
- 2 tablespoons water

In blender, combine basil, Parmesan, oil, salt, and water and puree until smooth. To store, spoon into a small container and top with a few tablespoons of olive oil. Cover and refrigerate for up to 1 week.

EACH SERVING: ABOUT 52 CALORIES, 1G PROTEIN, 0G CARBOHYDRATE, 5G TOTAL FAT (1G SATURATED), 2MG CHOLESTEROL, 119MG SODIUM.

TIP

While traditionally pesto is made with basil leaves, other herbs can be thrown into the mix for different flavors, whether that's dill, cilantro, or even fennel fronds.

Salsa Verde

Our recipe for Italian green sauce makes a terrific spread for fresh mozzarella and tomato sandwiches.

ACTIVE TIME: 15 MINUTES **TOTAL TIME:** 15 MINUTES **MAKES:** 1 CUP

- 1 garlic clove, cut in half
- ¼ teaspoon salt
- 2 cups packed fresh flat-leaf parsley leaves (about 3 bunches)
- ⅓ cup olive oil
- 3 tablespoons capers, drained
- 3 tablespoons fresh lemon juice
- 1 teaspoon Dijon mustard
- ⅛ teaspoon coarsely ground black pepper

In blender, combine garlic, salt, parsley, oil, capers, lemon juice, mustard, and pepper and blend until finely chopped. Transfer to small bowl. If not using sauce right away, cover and refrigerate up to 3 days.

EACH TABLESPOON: ABOUT 60 CALORIES, 0G PROTEIN, 1G CARBOHYDRATE, 6G TOTAL FAT (1G SATURATED), 0MG CHOLESTEROL, 140MG SODIUM.

Index

Note: Page numbers in **bold** indicate category overviews. Page numbers in *italics* indicate photos of recipes located apart from recipe.

Photography Credits

Chris Bain: 2, 13, 16, 26, 35, 36, 47, 60, 63, 66

Getty Images: Alexandra Grablewsk, 86; Jasmina, 51

Raymond Hom: 9, 103

iStockphoto: AbbieImages, 14; AlterYourReality , 50; Sedneva Anna, 40; Kaan Ates, 18; Bedo, 112; Bluestocking, 41; Hanis, 49; iSailorr, 90; Peng Li, 83 (water); LuVo, 76; Maakenzi, 94; Jul Nichols, 38 (chocolate syrup); Nkbimages, 72; Joanna Pecha, 25; PixelBay, 71; Ranplett, 53; Roxana Ro, 83 (sugar); Syolacan, 105; Tarek El Sombati, 117

Rita Maas: 116

Kate Mathis: 6, 10, 31

Johnny Miller: 100

Theresa Raffetto: 19, 32, 69, 70, 80, 91, 92, 95, 115, 121

Kate Sears: 108

Shutterstock: Andrjuss, 24; Teresa Azevedo, 123; Mongolka , 79; Kim Nguyen (banana) 38; Saiko3p, 29; Alex Staroseltsev, 23; vblinov, 8

Stockfood: Chris Alack, 56; Rob Fiocca Photography, 85; Foodgrafix, 52; Lars Ranek: 42; Gräfe & Unzer Verlag/Peter Schulte, 59; Anthony Tieuli, 73; Stephanie Weaver, 55

Studio D: Philip Friedman, 7

FRONT and BACK COVER: Chris Bain

Metric Conversion Charts

The recipes that appear in this cookbook use the standard United States method for measuring liquid and dry or solid ingredients (teaspoons, tablespoons, and cups). The information on this chart is provided to help cooks outside the U.S. successfully use these recipes. All equivalents are approximate.

METRIC EQUIVALENTS FOR DIFFERENT TYPES OF INGREDIENTS

STANDARD CUP	FINE POWDER (e.g. flour)	GRAIN (e.g. rice)	GRANULAR (e.g. sugar)	LIQUID SOLIDS (e.g. butter)	LIQUID (e.g. milk)
¾	105 g	113 g	143 g	150 g	180 ml
⅔	93 g	100 g	125 g	133 g	160 ml
½	70 g	75 g	95 g	100 g	120 ml
⅓	47 g	50 g	63 g	67 g	80 ml
¼	35 g	38 g	48 g	50 g	60 ml
⅛	18 g	19 g	24 g	25 g	30 ml

USEFUL EQUIVALENTS FOR LIQUID INGREDIENTS BY VOLUME

¼ tsp	=									1 ml
½ tsp	=									2 ml
1 tsp	=									5 ml
3 tsp	=	1 tbls	=				½ fl oz	=		15 ml
		2 tbls	=	⅛ cup	=		1 fl oz	=		30 ml
		4 tbls	=	¼ cup	=		2 fl oz	=		60 ml
		5⅓ tbls	=	⅓ cup	=		3 fl oz	=		80 ml
		8 tbls	=	½ cup	=		4 fl oz	=		120 ml
		10⅔ tbls	=	⅔ cup	=		5 fl oz	=		160 ml
		12 tbls	=	¾ cup	=		6 fl oz	=		180 ml
		16 tbls	=	1 cup	=		8 fl oz	=		240 ml
		1 pt	=	2 cups	=		16 fl oz	=		480 ml
		1 qt	=	4 cups	=		32 fl oz	=		960 ml
							33 fl oz	=		1000 ml = 1 L

USEFUL EQUIVALENTS FOR DRY INGREDIENTS BY WEIGHT

(To convert ounces to grams, multiply the number of ounces by 30.)

1 oz	=	1⁄16 lb	=	30 g
2 oz	=	¼ lb	=	120 g
4 oz	=	½ lb	=	240 g
8 oz	=	¾ lb	=	360 g
16 oz	=	1 lb	=	480 g

USEFUL EQUIVALENTS FOR COOKING/OVEN TEMPERATURES

	Fahrenheit	*Celsius*	*Gas Mark*
Freeze Water	32° F	0° C	
Room Temperature	68° F	20° C	
Boil Water	212° F	100° C	
Bake	325° F	160° C	3
	350° F	180° C	4
	375° F	190° C	5
	400° F	200° C	6
	425° F	220° C	7
	450° F	230° C	8
Broil			Grill

USEFUL EQUIVALENTS LENGTH

(To convert inches to centimeters, multiply the number of inches by 2.5.)

1 in	=					2.5 cm
6 in	=	½ ft	=			15 cm
12 in	=	1 ft	=			30 cm
36 in	=	3 ft	=	1 yd	=	90 cm
40 in	=					100 cm = 1 m

THE GOOD HOUSEKEEPING TRIPLE-TEST PROMISE

At *Good Housekeeping*, we want to make sure that every recipe we print works in any oven, with any brand of ingredient, no matter what. That's why, in our test kitchens at the **Good Housekeeping Research Institute**, we go all out: We test each recipe at least three times—and, often, several more times after that.

When a recipe is first developed, one member of our team prepares the dish, and we judge it on these criteria: It must be **delicious**, **family-friendly**, **healthy**, and **easy to make**.

1. The recipe is then tested several more times to fine-tune the flavor and ease of preparation, always by the same team member, using the same equipment.

2. Next, another team member follows the recipe as written, **varying the brands of ingredients** and **kinds of equipment**. Even the types of stoves we use are changed.

3. A third team member repeats the whole process **using yet another set of equipment** and **alternative ingredients**. By the time the recipes appear on these pages, they are guaranteed to work in any kitchen, including yours. **We promise**.